The Undeniable Strength of a Woman

VISIONARY AUTHOR

Kimmoly K LaBoo

ISBN-13: 978-1-954609-39-6

For information regarding special discounts for bulk purchases contact the Publisher:

LaBoo Publishing Enterprise, LLC
staff@laboopublishing.com
www.laboopublishing.com

All information is solely considered as the point of view of the authors.

Scripture quotations marked (NIV) are taken from the Holy Bible, New International Version®, NIV®. Copyright © 1973, 1978, 1984, 2011 by Biblica, Inc.™ Used by permission of Zondervan. All rights reserved worldwide. www.zondervan.com

Scripture quotations marked ESV are from the Holy Bible, English Standard Version, copyright © 2001 by Crossway Bibles, a publishing ministry of Good News Publishers. Used by permission. All rights reserved.

The Holy Bible, King James Version. Cambridge Edition: 1769; King James Bible Online, 2019. www.kingjamesbibleonline.org.

Scripture quotations marked (NLT) are taken from the Holy Bible, New Living Translation, copyright ©1996, 2004, 2015 by Tyndale House Foundation. Used by permission of Tyndale House Publishers, Inc., Carol Stream, Illinois 60188. All rights reserved.

When It's All Said and Done by Kimmoly LaBoo previously printed in Living Your Vision and Purpose (Bruised But Not Broken) – Used by permission of Professional Woman Network. www.pwnbooks.com.

Contents

Introduction

The undeniable strength of a woman—just the thought of that brings so many scenarios to mind of heroic women I've known in my lifetime. Not heroic in the sense of rescuing someone from a burning building, but more like the countless women I have seen battle breast cancer, or single moms who have struggled tirelessly to provide for their children, or the women who have survived abuse, rape, molestation or domestic violence. Then there are the women who have cared for a spouse or parent battling illness or raised a child with special needs. We also have moms who are fighting to show up after the heartbreaking loss of a child. The lists are endless.

This past summer I had the opportunity to meet Stedman Graham—yes, Oprah's man, although he is so much more than that title. He was the mentor of our mastermind group and had travelled to Arizona to pour into us as entrepreneurs. He spoke to us about leadership and identity and how we embrace and show up in our purpose. I was so intrigued by his compassion for women, his effortless conversation, and his subtle strength. At the end of our session it was time to move to another room for lunch. As we all piled into the room many passed by the first table where Stedman, his host for the day, and our mastermind coach sat. I believe they assumed the table was reserved. However, when my business bestie and I finally made it through the door, a lady in front of us asked if the remaining seats at the table were taken, to which our coach replied, "No, you can sit here." With that, we quickly jumped at the opportunity to dine with Stedman and be part of a more intimate conversation over our meal.

We all got our plates and drinks and the conversation ensued. Stedman had earlier in our session talked about knowing your purpose and having all other decisions you make align with your end goal. He shared how he knew there were certain things he could not or would not do because he knew they would cause him to deviate from the end goal for his life. This made me ponder something. As I listened to him talk during lunch, I got up the nerve to ask him a question. I wanted to know what his thoughts were about his theory of not doing certain things that might deter you from your ultimate purpose, balanced against the message that is prevalent in society today of the "Just do you" culture. While answering my question Stedman started talking about the role of women in society and how much we deal with, and the weight of our decisions. He further stated how women are the backbone of so many things, the ones who pour into our children, imparting morals and values, the ones who nurture and care for, the ones who support our men and teach our children.

As Stedman was rattling off this enormous list of responsibilities that sounded like the weight of the world on a woman's shoulders, I could feel myself fighting back tears. I was doing okay at concealing my emotions, or so I thought, until our coach looked at me and asked, "What is happening? What is coming up for you?" She could see that I was on the verge of tears. I tried to respond, but instead of releasing words, I released a river of tears that I'd been holding on to for months. The table went silent, as no one knew what the heck was going on. I was literally sitting in front of Stedman Graham doing the Oprah ugly cry. I still can't believe I did that. There were people rubbing my back and handing me tissues. Geez, I knew I had to pull it together. I took a deep breath and tried to explain myself. As he was talking about how great we are as women, I thought about my oldest sister, who had just a couple of months prior lost her son, my nephew, to murder in Baltimore City. I had put on my brave face to support her and had masked my own pain because I felt like I shouldn't be crying harder than her because, after all, he was her only child. All I was thinking about in that moment was how hard she had tried to successfully raise him, to impart wisdom, guidance, and a godly foundation and yet her son still ended up being killed at an early age. Stedman was so gracious in that moment, and once I finished sharing the conversation at the table continued. I will forever be grateful for the compassion he and everyone else at the table exhibited in that moment.

That whole encounter with Stedman Graham is what inspired this project. Realizing the weight of the mantle that we carry as women was so profound. It's not like I didn't already know, but hearing a man articulate it so eloquently really sparked a firm desire in me to highlight and celebrate the undeniable strength of a woman. Even as we worked to complete this project, we all faced enormous challenges in the midst of it. We hope sharing our stories will inspire more women to open up and share their experiences and how they have overcome to further uplift and encourage others.

With love and compassion,

Kimmoly

The Undeniable Strength of a Woman

The Undeniable Strength of a Woman
   runs deeply within her soul.
The Undeniable Strength of a Woman
   walks with ease and simple elegance.
The Undeniable Strength of a Woman
   wears a regal crown and adjusts accordingly.
The Undeniable Strength of a Woman
   is enrobed in peace, love, faith, hope, and joy.
The Undeniable Strength of a Woman
   has honor.
The Undeniable Strength of a Woman
   carries the weight of the World on her shoulders.
The Undeniable Strength of a Woman
   displays vulnerability.
The Undeniable Strength of a Woman
   loves herself deeply.
The Undeniable Strength of a Woman
   inhales deeply and exhales slowly.
The Undeniable Strength of a Woman
   projects her truth, even if it means going against
   the grain.
The Undeniable Strength of a Woman
   taps into a divine force for strength.
The Undeniable Strength of a Woman
   overcomes life's trials and tribulations.

The Undeniable Strength of a Woman
    pushes through adversity and perseveres.
The Undeniable Strength of a Woman
    triumphs during challenging times.
The Undeniable Strength of a Woman
    is a woman who walks with authority, purpose,
    and courage.
The Undeniable Strength of a Woman
    has a rooted connection to history.
The Undeniable Strength of a Woman
    has the power of influence; her power spans the
    whole generation of women, present and future.
The Undeniable Strength of a Woman
    shares infinite wisdom as a badge of honor.
The Undeniable Strength of a Woman
    is an intricate masterpiece, woven together like a
    textured quilt.
The Undeniable Strength of a Woman
    has many layers about her, layers that tell a
    different story—a story like many.
The Undeniable Strength of a Woman
    births many stories.
The Undeniable Strength of a Woman
    gathers strength from other women; women
    who share similar stories of despair, loss, pain,
    heartache, sorrow, BUT also love, triumph,
    perseverance, wisdom, and integrity.
The Undeniable Strength of a Woman
    is RESILIENT and WITHSTANDS the test of time!

Lovingly Written by a Woman of Undeniable Strength
*Monique Johnson

Shanina L Jones is a Mom, Chef, and Entrepreneur. Shanina started her college education off at her favorite HBCU, North Caroline A&T State University. She later relocated to Georgia and graduated from Le Cordon Bleu in Culinary Arts. After working in the culinary field Shanina found that her passion extended to not only cooking but teaching people about the power of eating right as well.

Shanina attended and received her certification from Hippocrates Health Institute in West Palm Beach Florida. That's where she really learned about healthy eating and how to heal your body with food. Although no longer in the kitchen professionally, Shanina caters many dinners for organizations. She is now the Chief Operating Officer at the family run brokerage, where she teaches people about financial prosperity. She has hopes to one day open a facility where she and others can help people work on all five areas of prosperity: Spiritual, Mental, Social, Physical and Financial. It is her greatest desire to help families worldwide to grow in their walk, their talk, and their giving.

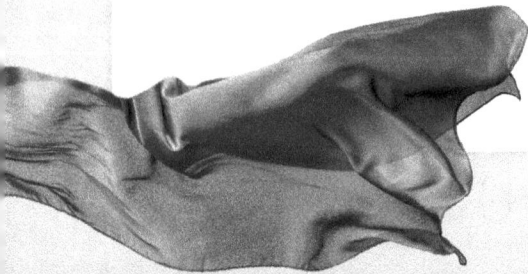

Putting His Super on My Natural:
Who do you turn to when your strength has run out?

Shanina Jones

What is strength? The Webster dictionary defines it as the capacity for exertion or endurance.

As women we wear many hats. We are moms, daughters, granddaughters, caregivers, nurturers, and providers. We often have to be strong for so many people, including ourselves. But what happens when our strength runs out? Who do we turn to for that strength? The word of God says, "But those who hope in the Lord will renew their strength…They will run and not grow weary, they will walk and not be faint" (Isaiah 40:31, NIV). Over the last few years my strength has been tested more than ever.

Growing up I was always surrounded by some of the strongest women I know. They have all shown me strength in so many ways. I have two very strong grandmothers. My grandmother on my mom's side had nine children. That right there is a special kind of strength because I have one and I am ready to pull my hair out, so I can't imagine having to raise nine! My grandmother on my dad's side only had two kids but she was the caregiver of the entire family. Both women are very different, but they taught me the power in the strength of love and in God.

I have five aunts between both sides of my families. All these women are very strong in their own way. They raised kids; they are there for their families; they have had to face many different adversities and have gone through all of them gracefully.

My aunt on my dad's side has had rheumatoid arthritis since she was younger and though many doubted she would be able to do things, she has proven them wrong. She has shown me the power of determination.

Last but definitely not least, I was raised by the strongest person I know, my mother. She has had to face many things that would have taken most out, but she faced them and never backed down and came out stronger than ever. She had to raise a child when she didn't have much. She started a business in finance and when most doubted her and turned their backs, she kept going and built it to a multimillion-dollar business. She went from having to catch buses everywhere to owning multiple cars. She went from healthy one day to stage four cancer the next day and back to healthy and still providing for her family through it all. She taught me the power of the strength to never give up.

By now you're probably thinking with all this strength that I was raised around, why would I be talking about what to do when your strength runs out? Simply because I was looking at them from the outside in. I didn't see what they did to regain their strength when they were low. I didn't understand how much they leaned on God until I had to do that for myself. April 30, 2018 was a turning point in my life. Before then my life was pretty good. I traveled; I lived in different states; I was going out and just enjoying my life. I had a relationship with God and although that was perfect, I wasn't. But everything changed the day I went on life support. Since then my life is still good but it has definitely been a rollercoaster of emotions and events. I went from laughing to life support to finding out I had an illness that most doctors don't even recognize as an illness. After beating that, I found out I was pregnant and it was a high-risk pregnancy. During my pregnancy my dad's health started declining and he was in and out of the hospital. I am an only child and he never married, so he relied so much on me, and I felt like it was my duty to be there for him even when I was put on bed rest. My daughter was born at 25 weeks and 6 days. She spent 75 days in NICU. While she was in the hospital my dad was also in a different hospital. I would go from one hospital to the next just about every day. When I look back on that time of my life, I am still amazed that I made it through. But I know that it was because of my strength. I have always battled with self-esteem issues and I didn't view myself as a strong woman. But 2018 and 2019 really showed me how strong I was.

I had to learn to lean on what was taught to me growing up. I was always taught that the Lord is my shepherd and my shield and that no weapons formed against me would prosper. But up until these years I never fully understood what my mom and my family really meant when they said those words. We as Christians can become such scripture reciters. We know scripture word for word. But do we ever really mean them? Or do we even know what they truly mean? I know I didn't and at times I still questioned if I truly understood them until I actually had to live them. Between 2018 and 2019, I felt so alone. Even though I had an amazing village around me, I still felt lost! It felt like every weapon formed against me was truly about to prosper. I felt so weak, so inadequate. But God showed me that he had me, that when I was weak, he put his arms around me and made my natural strength super.

I thought things were getting better. My daughter was doing good. My dad was doing better. He was finally home. But then my dad's health started taking a turn. I then became a caregiver of not only a newborn but my dad too. My dad was always the life of the party. He was outgoing and lovable. I watched as his sickness sucked that life out of him. I would pray for him to get better more than I would for me. I wanted my daddy back! I would try to be the positive light in his darkness of sickness. I would remind him of how awesome he was. I would have him talk about what he wanted to do when he got better. We would often talk about taking trips together or going to different restaurants. As time went on my dad would be in and out of nursing homes and hospitals. I would be running from one place to the other to make sure he had what he needed, while also being a single parent to a newborn.

After about a year in and out of hospitals, my dad finally got to come home. But, I was so excited. But I quickly learned that meant I would become a full-time caregiver. At that time, I had a one-year-old, and my own health started to affect me. I don't want it to seem like I am complaining. I want you to see what happens when it seems like so much is coming at you at one time and you feel like you can't handle anymore. Because at this point my dad was wheelchair bound, I had to make sure he ate and took his medicine and I had to change him. Whenever he called me I would drop what I was doing to rush to him. It was not easy. I cried many days because I did not know if I could handle it. I wanted to be there for him, but it was costing me physically, emotionally and mentally. I wanted to be the rock, the person who gave him hope of better days. But I needed all of that myself.

My health started to be affected. It became harder for me to walk, to go up and down stairs, and hard to lift things. I remember one day I went to lift my child up and that was hard. So I finally went to see what was wrong with me and after testing, I found out that I had Rheumatoid Arthritis. Like seriously! Another thing, God? I was crushed. I knew about RA because my aunt has had it pretty much all her life. Yes, she lives a good life but I have seen the pain and the limitations that it cost her, and I did not want that for me. I couldn't go through this. I was a single mother. I had a child to care for, and I had a father to care for. I did not want someone to have to care for me. "Seriously, God! Why would you put this on me now? It's not a good time." Those were the conversations I had with God. "How can I take on this when I already have so much to take care of? I'm not strong enough for this!" And God said to me, "Yes, alone you are not strong enough but in me you are supernatural." This reminds me of another verse that we learn early in life, Philippians 4:13, NIV: "I can do all this through him who gives me strength." We cite the verse often. But do we ever truly believe this verse or do we know the meaning of it? I can do all things does not mean that it won't be hard or that you won't feel weak but it is in those hard and weak moments that you seek him more. When your strength runs out you seek him to give you more strength. This is when he puts his super on your natural.

On those days when my dad was really sick and needed me to do so much for him and I was in so much pain, God put his super on my natural. Those days when my daughter had doctor appointments or was sick and all I wanted to do was curl up in bed because I was exhausted, God put his super on my natural. I had to learn to lean on him, to understand that he is always with me. As women we can sometimes go on autopilot to make sure that we are there for our loved ones, but do we ever stop and thank God for putting our super cape on us? Because if he didn't we wouldn't be able to do what we do in this world, let alone in our families.

With all that was going on with me I still had to take care of my dad and my child and be there for my grandparents and help my mom in her business. My mom has a saying for when people say they have a lot going on. She says, "The answer is D. All the above." That saying basically means to figure it out! We as women are really good at figuring things out. I had to figure out how to be all the roles that they needed me to be.

They needed me and I had to be there for them, even when it wasn't easy emotionally. Seeing my dad change before my eyes was very hard. I saw his health declining and his anger and bitterness strength. I would always try to be positive for him and keep him happy, but you learn that you cannot make someone happy if they do not have happiness in them. My dad started to become angry with the world and take it out on the closest one to him, which was me. Sickness can make someone angry and bitter and we as women can sometimes take the brunt of it. We have to take the negative comments and misappropriated anger and still take care of these people. Even though I was experiencing this, and what my dad would say hurt, I still would try to remain positive for him. When my dad went back into the hospital, I would still try to remain positive. But I could feel that he was giving up. Thanksgiving 2020 would be that last time I would see my dad alive. He went back into the hospital shortly after and would never come back home. My dad died May of 2021, and I was so angry. I was angry at myself because I had opportunities to go see him and I did not because in his last months he wasn't the nicest person and I wanted to protect my mental health. I should have done more. I should have been there more. I was angry at him because I felt like my daddy gave up. Why would he do that? Did he not know that I still needed my daddy? Who would walk me down the aisle and give me away? I wasn't ready for this. I couldn't handle this. I literally felt my heart break into pieces. How could my life go on without him? I felt weak again. How was I going to plan a funeral when I wanted to curl up and die myself? But God again put his super on my natural. I had to lean on him and pray for him to give me the strength! I had to be strong for my family.

Losing my dad was the hardest thing I ever had to face in my life. We still had so much life to live together, so many memories to make. But now I had to learn a new way of life.

By this time someone might say whew, this has been a lot, but I haven't even finished. Now during this time of talking about my dad I had not mentioned that my father's mother suffered a stroke and was on life support. So while I was caring for my dad, I thought we would have to bury my grandma. But my grandmother is a fighter and she pulled through, went to rehab and eventually came home. She had been home a few months by the time my dad passed but she still required 24-hour care. On my mom's side my grandparents started having issues and needing extra help. I was still grieving my dad but I had to be there for my child and my family. I had to start helping my aunt with my grandmother and my mom with my grandparents. Every week I would spend two nights with my grandmother, helping her and making sure she ate, took her medication and was changed. When my aunt called, I would be there. I felt I was in the same cycle that I was in with my dad. I am an only child and only grandchild. I felt that I had to be there. I wanted to be there even when I physically did not feel up to it. I would push through the pain to be wherever my family needed me to be because I love them.

I was with my grandmother faithfully for the whole year after my dad's passing. Through all the hospital visits, through the sick days and nights, through my aunt being in an accident and being bedridden and having to help her as well—it just felt like so much had been placed on me, but I kept praying, God help me. And he did! Even when I thought I wasn't doing enough he would send messages in many forms to tell me I was.

The last days of my grandmother's life were really a miracle to see. My grandmother went into the hospital for breathing issues and while there she had another massive stroke. I knew this one she wouldn't recover from. I prayed to God that he'd grant my grandmother peace but what I didn't know was that she would have unfinished business to take care of before she left peacefully. During the time of her stroke my daughter started having really high fevers. She was so sick that I had to take her into the hospital a couple of times. On the third time they admitted her and had to put her on IVs for severe dehydration. I was taking care of a sick child and dealing with the transition of my grandmother. It was one of the hardest weeks emotionally and mentally. The day we took my grandmother off the ventilator; the hospital had to put Skylar on oxygen. I don't know how to explain it because in those few days it felt like there was an exchange of spirit between my daughter and my grandmother. I would watch Skylar sleep and it was as if she was communicating in her sleep to someone. I didn't know what it was or how to explain it until the day she was released from the hospital. I was leaving the hospital when I got the call that my grandmother had finally transitioned. All I could do was cry. Some of my tears were the sadness of losing my grandmother but the tears were also because even in her last moments I felt like my grandma used her last strength to make sure my baby was ok, and the moment Skylar was released from the hospital my grandmother took her last breath.

These last few years of my life have been a rollercoaster of emotions. I've dealt with two deaths, two diagnoses of illness and premature childbirth. But through it all I have learned so much about myself. I have learned that I am more than capable to do it all with my village and, most importantly, with God by my side. I've learned to lean on God, because as women we are very strong but at some point our strength does run out and when it does, we have to lean on God to put his super on our natural strength.

The moral of the story is, when I didn't have any more to give, God showed up and gave me all that I needed. It's in our weakness that he is the strongest.

So do not fear, for I am with you;
do not be dismayed, for I am your God.
I will strengthen you and help you;
I will uphold you with my righteous right hand.
Isaiah 41:10, NIV

Amen.

"Each time a woman
stands up for herself,
she stands up for all
women."

- Maya Angelou

Larvetricus Harris is known by many as Pastor Vee or Coach Vee. Regardless of her title or what many may call her, she is a young woman who has learned how to overcome many difficulties. Larvetricus is influential in affecting everyone around her to grow in all aspects of life, with the notion of challenging individuals to never become paralyzed in their journey of life.

Larvetricus is a contributing author of "The Mom In Me 2" and the author of, "A Child's Cry in the Shadow," which shares the testimony of her overcoming many obstacles from a young age to some of her adult life.

To better educate herself, Larvetricus obtained an Associate Degree of Arts in Business Administration through Strayer University and has obtained Certification as a Master Life Coach. As a wife, mother, and friend, through God, she has coined the phrase with understanding "Just because the door is broken, does not mean it does not open…" We just have to find the ability to discover the strength to look for an opening. In all, Larvetricus makes it her business to guide, lead, and coach individuals into any possibility that presents itself.

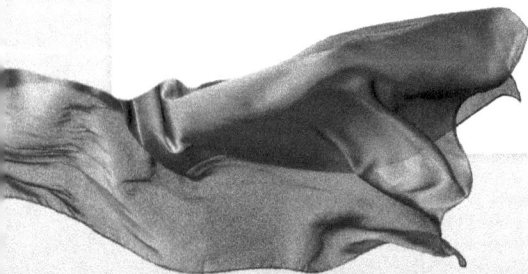

Not Built to Break

Larvetricus Harris

As I sit under the sun and observe the home I was raised in as a child, the yard is nicely manicured, just like he would have loved it. My mind rewinds back to the time that my cousins and I would shoot basketball on a makeshift rim made of a bucket. Just like yesterday, I can hear my father screaming, "Get outside and practice your shots." I was just getting home from school at that time, and I did not feel like shooting ball, but my father never took no for an answer. Rain, sleet, or snow, I had to learn to perfect my shot! Regardless of what I wanted to do or how I felt, I had to learn how to rise to the occasion. It reminded me of what was called Michael Jordan's Flu Game. Jordan found himself as sick as a dog in the 1997 final playoffs with the Utah Jazz. Just picture it: Jordan had absolutely no energy to play this game; he stated that he felt as though he was going to pass out. He was tripping over his own feet; he was sweating profusely; no matter what he did, he could not pull it together. Every single shot in the 1st, 2nd, and 3rd quarter was a total struggle, so Jordan began to pace himself as much as he could to continue to be who he needed to be for the team. Shot after shot nothing hit, sportscasters were commenting on this being one of the lowest scoring games they had seen from Jordan. Jordan continued to pace himself and something snapped in the 4th quarter for Jordan. Regardless of how sick he felt, he was able to pull on some type of strength to pull off the last shot to win the championship game for the Bulls. That game reminded me of my dad. He would always refer to basketball when trying to display to me what strength looked like and how I should face pressure, even if I did not want to face it. "Larvetricus, I really care what goes on in your life," he would say. "Just learn to pace yourself, while never allowing your opponent to know how you feel. Daughter, embrace life and respond by allowing your shot to speak for itself." Of course, he did not say that as nicely, but I never realized how basketball would play out in my life until I was reminded of that game. For the last seven years, I have had some fourth quarter experiences that could have taken me out. Life has literally knocked the life out of me!

On your mark, get set, go! In my mind, I hear the referee blow his whistle each morning as my feet hit the floor. This statement rings in my ears like an alarm clock that has no snooze button. *On your mark:* I begin to filter through the rolodex of tasks, events or objectives that need to be completed by end of the day, week, month, or year. *Get set:* I steady myself and breathe, trying to figure out how in the world I am going to accomplish anything and everything that has been scheduled for me to complete. *Go:* I take off on the journey of life, trying to brave and maneuver through each season that comes my way. In October 2015, October 2019, and November 2021, I received calls that caused me to pause as my world was flooded like a hurricane with the pain that my loved ones were no longer taking space on this earth.

In October 2015, I was on my way to the soccer field to coach my little ones into a championship game when my cell phone rang and a voice on the other end stated that my sister had passed away in her sleep. My sister and I had a relationship more like a mother and daughter would have, based on the circumstances of our past with our father and mother. When I received the call that she was gone, a ton of bricks hit my heart. It was like something was holding my breath hostage. For ten minutes, my thoughts were swimming around in my mind, trying to figure out what in the world I was going to do. When asked by my husband if I wanted to go home, I responded, "No, I have a game to win." This question snapped me back into the now and I knew as I looked toward that soccer field, seeing the little kids, I had to push myself to continue. Individuals who heard the situation surrounded me with prayer, not knowing that was the energy I needed to move a little farther. Standing on that soccer field watching nine-year-old girls and boys run up and down the field felt like a lifetime, but it was the escape I needed just for that moment. A portion of my heart was dangling like a hangnail, but I had to find a way to muster up enough strength to smile and hold others through this trying time. It was not an easy journey with my family, especially watching my father and mother deal with the passing of their baby girl. I found myself taking every arrow while trying to stop the arrows from hitting others. My strength was being developed in ways that a basketball game could never explain.

Just when I thought I was getting my groove back from the death of my sister, my father called me the Sunday before Labor Day in 2018 at four o'clock in the morning and told me he had been diagnosed with stage four pancreatic cancer. Silence muted my voice; I was quiet on the phone, as I listened to my heartbeat trying to escape my chest. My father broke the stillness by stating, "I know your silence and don't worry, God has a plan." He began to reference basketball and it was that that once again snapped me back into the now. From the time of his diagnosis, I had a wonderful, trying year with him and at 5:48 in the morning as I was getting ready for work on October 14, 2019, I received a call that my father took his last breath peacefully and he was no longer with us. *Geez,* I yelled to myself as loudly as I could as I stood in worship with my hands lifted. *First my sister and now my father.* My father constantly made the statement throughout the year while going back and forth to chemo, "It's all or nothing…" Whatever you do in life, you either give it your all or just don't do anything. And as I eulogized him, it was those words that gave me the fire to encourage everyone at the funeral to take life, relationships, and time a little more seriously. It is either all or nothing!

I am not saying it is easy. I am thinking and echoing the voices that I often hear people talk about: God is preparing me for something I cannot handle right now…But wait, life did not stop there. On November 24, 2021, I was in the grocery store purchasing turkeys for our annual church's turkey drive for Thanksgiving. My cell phone was ringing and at first, I thought I would call my aunt back, but something was pressing me to answer the phone. Not knowing what she wanted, I never thought I would hear the words that came out of her mouth. I talk to my aunt frequently, but I knew when I heard her voice something was wrong. "Larvetricus," she said with a low-spirited voice, "they found your mother dead in her apartment." My heart dropped into my feet as warm tears ran down my face, like a faucet that was dripping. This call was like the call that I received of my sister's very unexpected death. For the life of me, I never in a million years would have thought I would receive that call two years after the call about my father. *This is jacked up,* I thought as I silently yelled to myself, *Now what, God? I'm the only one left.* I felt like my feet were locked in place as I stood in the middle of a grocery store with my oldest son staring at me, while I told him that his grandmother was no longer living. I felt like I was pinned inside this invisible cage. I heard my father's voice: "Larvetricus, get back in the game, don't allow this pain to paralyze you, you got this!" As I was still trying to resonate those words, my son said, "Ma, you good?" Something snapped as I heard his voice and the doors to that invisible cage swung open as I stepped out and thought to myself, *My son is watching my response to this pain.*

Two days from Thanksgiving, and I am far from feeling thankful. After serving, I finished that night resting in my tears. It wasn't until Friday morning that my aunt called and stated that my mother's body had been released. I immediately gathered my things and took the first, quickest flight to Tennessee. As soon as I arrived at my destination, we hit the ground running. While cleaning my mother's apartment with my aunt and cousins, I discovered her journals and as I read them, it was her words that gave me the strength to eulogize her. Line after line, in sync with her journey, I learned that no matter what she went through she made a proclamation that "Still I Rise..." My word! As I read the memoirs of her life that she never chatted about, I instantly knew at that moment that I inherited my strength from her. Wow!

With all that strength invested and being birthed out of me, it still leaves me to wonder why God left me here. How much more can I take? Though we were blood related, each one of their deaths affected me differently, but the pain of loneliness, frustration, anger, and brokenness was the same. I often hear individuals quote, "God will never put more on you than you can bear." But I am now wondering exactly how much more I can take. My heart is empty, thumbing for answers that only God can give. Why in the blue bonkers did God leave me here to continue to deal with the aftermath of the pain of my family being absent from this earth?

I often feel like a smorgasbord that life picks from and chooses daily routines that challenge my existence. You talk about being a strong profound woman—oh, how I wish strength was a vitamin that anyone could pop in their mouth each day and be renewed with just a swallow. Yet strength is not anything that can be easily digested. I have learned and am learning that strength, is a will of the mind. A will to continue, regardless of...

Each circumstance that I have gone and/or suffered through was like weights being lifted to make my muscles stronger. Instead of the muscles, my weights are causing my mind and my will to become stronger. Yes, I cry, yell, and say some things many in my profession will not agree with. There are times I would love to run and hide like the bear that hibernates during the winter. But that 'will to' continues, regardless of...it's that will to go through the process of healing, even if you have to escape for a season.

Every so often, individuals remind me that what does not break you will only make you stronger. A quote by Dr. Seuss stated,

"When something bad happens you have three choices. You can either let it define you, let it destroy you, or you can let it strengthen you." Somebody please tell me, where in the world do you find that type of stamina to keep moving when things hurt? How do you let pain build you? All my life I thought I received my strength from my father. Yes, my twin, my dad taught me through the illustrations of basketball how to keep it moving. He never allowed me to become paralyzed, stuck in a space that did not cause me to look forward. Not only that, but tears were not an option around him. The toughness of strength was displayed out of him. But my mother taught me the side of strength through tears, while smiling. Even though she left me and my sister at a very young age, I watched her as much as possible throughout my life. As previously stated, it was not until I read the chronicles of her life that I understood, even more, that strength is a choice. My mother moved in silence, and yet she rose through so many obstacles that should have killed or destroyed her. She stated in one of her journals, "The sting from the hand of him has caused my tears to break like a levee holding an ocean in place. Instead of hiding I will choose to cry and smile at the same time." My God! Those words, when I read them, vibrated within my eardrums like an echo being heard from miles away. It was like I heard my mother speaking directly to me: "Lar-vetri-cus, when the pain hits you like an earthquake and shakes the very foundation of your being, choose to embrace the pain and continue to lift your hands to Jehovah, knowing that everything works together for your good. Sweetheart, smile," she would say. "Don't let life define you, but move silently as the world sees and hears your beauty, your strength through your actions…"

It is easy to lean on others for muscle. It is easy to say you have something when nothing has tested the very thing that you depend on to keep you stable in certain situations. And though I had those experiences to help guide and lead me on this journey in life, I am now learning how to stand on my own and really trust God through the process. Really learning to put my hope in Him when everything seems to be stripped away. Yes, even believing Him for the impossible, when doors are being shut in your face with your eyes wide open. If I can muster up a modicum of strength, eventually I will birth out plenty. My definition of strength is embracing the now, while maneuvering through the process, not becoming fixated in today to live tomorrow.

Though I constantly told myself that I would not let anything paralyze me, when my sister, father, and mother passed, I discovered that I was in a season where my faith was very strong, but my strength is gone. It was completely depleted! Yes, I preached and encouraged many, but now I found myself in a corner looking for the words to encourage myself. I felt like everything I was doing was out of a place of emptiness. How in the world do you speak life through a multitude of hurt? How do you speak life when it seems as though the one who gives life took life from you? How do you totally trust God without pause, when it seems as though He took life? I do not believe in coincidences; I believe everything and everyone has a purpose and plan for our life that will eventually lead us into our destiny. I truly believe I serve an intentional God!

I thought that it was okay to suffer in a quiet place alone, to only cry tears behind a closed door and locked windows. So now, after all these years, I'm in a place where it seems as though my faith is on trial. Many nights, alone I pleaded with God not to wake me up. The weight of this life is weighing me down, like an anchor that holds a ship in place. At times I feel like a piece of a missing puzzle; within years everything, in a blink of an eye, is gone and I do not know where I fit in. Yet, I hear a small still voice that continues to push me forward: "Larvetricus, I did not create you to break!" I'm terrified in knowing why God is developing my faith and building my strength this way. Yet the person with the greatest vision is the individual that cannot see.

It does not matter who you are, the color of your skin, your gender, or your credentials, life is going to happen. Each person who was dear to my heart passed away in the fourth quarter of the year. Baby, the pressure was turned up and life was not joking nor playing games with me. The enemy was trying to use the pain of my loved ones to destroy me. But God has a way of building you in silence, so the enemy does not know what to attack. Somehow, I was able to maneuver and manage life as it happened. I am learning to face the process of grief, denial, anger, bargaining, depression, and acceptance. This means I have had to learn how to handle my emotions, manage my thoughts, and control my anger in order to execute the right response in any given situation.

I can remember being in preschool and kindergarten, and at that time the school required us to use jumbo pencils. You must keep in mind, as preschoolers, we were not familiar with holding items in our hands and writing. We had to learn how to adjust; we had to learn how much pressure to apply for words to be produced on paper; we had to learn our strength. So by them requiring us to use the jumbo pencils, it gave us the opportunity to learn and adjust. The teachers learned that the real big jumbo pencils would not easily break. They were able to endure the hardship or frustration of a preschooler or kindergartener learning how to write.

That jumbo pencil represents everything that you will have to face. The weird and unexplainable thing is at times you will be the jumbo pencil and preschooler at the same time. You must learn to hold every pain and calamity that happens in your life, while being that preschooler learning how to deal with the disappointments that it causes. You have to learn how to adjust and endure hardships and frustration, and maneuver through life as life happens all at the same time. It's like God is using grief to empty me and strengthen me all at the same time. From the process of talking, counseling, and journaling I learned that I am the same person, just with a shifted spirit. This grief has caused me to look at things from a different lens, to do things differently in my life, and not to wait to enjoy it. Through many tears and a whole lot of screaming, just like that pencil, no matter how much pressure is applied, I am not built to break!

"A woman is the full circle. Within her is the power to create, nurture and transform."

–Diane Mariechild

As a life balance coach and CEO of Profitable Productivity, LLC, Trasetta Washington partners with women executives and business owners to help them have it all without sacrificing what matters most. She shares strategies to embrace self-care as a way to optimize efficiency through trainings, workshops and speaking, as well as group and one-on-one coaching.

Trasetta has over 25 years of experience working in business operations management creating systems and processes and increasing individual productivity. After working for years 55+ hours a week, she took a leap of faith to build a life and career that complemented each other rather than competed. She is on a mission to help other successful women create the same thing through what she calls #balancedambition.

Trasetta is an engaging speaker and trainer, empowering attendees to move beyond simply hearing into implementing to experience the change they seek. In 2019, Trasetta received the Distinguished Alumni Award from her alma mater, Thomas University, from which she holds a Bachelor's degree in Social Work.

Trasetta is the proud parent of her adult daughter, Alexia. She is a breast cancer survivor, mentor to girls and respected leader. Trasetta is committed to showing others how to implement small daily actions to achieve their greatest dreams.

The Strength of Softness

Trasetta Washington

Words have multiple meanings. Often, we have a general idea of the definition of a word but may lack the full understanding of its meaning. Before I begin talking about true strength being softness, I'd like to review the many definitions of the word strong. These definitions are taken from the Oxford Dictionary.

Strong:

1. having the power to move heavy weights or perform other physically demanding tasks, possessing skills and qualities that create a likelihood of success.
2. able to withstand great force or pressure, not easily affected by disease or hardship, not easily disturbed, upset or affected.
3. very intense, not soft or muted, clear or prominent.

When we think about strength, we tend to look at it from two different lenses as it relates to the genders. For men, strength is usually centered around their physical ability. It speaks to a man's ability to use his physical body to accomplish tasks like lifting a heavy object or loosening a lid stuck on a jar. In contrast, when we look at the strength of a woman, the focus leans toward emotional fortitude. She is revered for her ability to persevere in the midst of multiple challenging life circumstances without "losing it."

Both of these applications of the word strength are accurate and can be used toward either gender when placed in similar situations. However, what is rarely looked at as strength is the ability to be soft. Most people think about softness as being weak. But what if true strength is the ability to remain soft in spite of difficult life circumstances, the ones that would typically harden you?

I've encountered so many women on my life journey who have become hard and cynical because of the difficult situations life has thrown their way. These women operate out of their masculine energy rather than their feminine energy. It may be as a result of sexual assault, molestation, abuse, racism, sexism, unfaithful romantic partners, or maybe even workplace inequities. Quite frankly, the majority of women experience all or most of these scenarios in their lifetime. Who could blame them for hardening their heart and putting up walls? I, myself, can check off several of these boxes. And to be frank, I followed the pattern of so many other women, allowing myself to close off and go through life on guard. I never knew what crisis might show up at any given time, so I did what I thought would protect me from being hurt. Unfortunately, this has caused me to also shut out people and opportunities that would likely add value to my life. Allow me to expound on this.

One example of emotional strength is when I faced a major health crisis. In 2014, at the age of 40, I was diagnosed with D.C.I.S. (ductal carcinoma in situ), an early form of breast cancer. Even though my prognosis was good, I still felt confronted by my own mortality. As I began to evaluate my life and think about the things I still wanted to experience, I realized I had been playing it safe. Now, don't get me wrong, I had a good life. Not great, but good. I wanted more, and I believed more was available. In order to pursue this more, it meant some changes had to be implemented. Though I was aware that I needed to make changes, actually implementing them was the challenging part.

I needed help to get through my treatment. Asking for help was viewed in my family as a sign of weakness. I can hear my mother's voice echoing in my mind when someone fails to follow through on a promise or commitment. She always says, "You can't depend on anyone else but yourself." I had no choice but to allow others to assist me in this particular situation. I simply couldn't do certain things on my own. By asking for help and receiving it, my perspective began to shift. I recognized this picture of strength was faulty, rooted in fear and trauma.

As my journey continued, I allowed bravery, boldness, and fortitude to manifest in my daily life. That looks like taking a chance on me by starting a business, investing in personal development, and opening up to the process of healing. By now, you're probably wondering what all of this has to do with softness. It's important for you to know the backstory in order to fully appreciate how I came to the revelation of the ability to be soft as true strength.

Over the course of the next six years, I did the work. As a result, I grew personally, professionally, emotionally, and spiritually. There was a downside for all of this growth, though, I must admit. I didn't do a good job of bringing my husband at the time along the journey with me. And the truth is, if you don't grow together, you grow apart.

Just a couple of months into the COVID-19 pandemic, my husband asked for a divorce. Even though I wasn't really happy in the marriage, I was devastated. I thought we were just going through a rough patch and would get through it. We spent the next year vacillating between ending things and trying to rebuild. Ultimately, we parted ways. Not too long after, I unexpectedly met someone new. We clicked instantly. Within a couple of months, I fell in love.

Surprised to be in such a wonderful relationship so quickly, I did my best to balance optimism with caution. Unfortunately, after six months, I discovered he was married. I was absolutely crushed. However, the demise of both of these relationships ended up serving as a catalyst for my healing journey. It is in this process of healing that I uncovered the concept of softness being a strength.

It would've been easy for me to put my walls back up and step into boss bitch energy. You know, where you go all in on career and only entertain a man or a woman (if that's your thing) to fulfill your physical desires, essentially shifting into your masculine energy. But I didn't do that. I made a conscious decision to remain open. I viewed both experiences as opportunities to learn about myself, grow and heal.

Let me tell you, it isn't an easy process. If you have attempted to heal yourself, you're well aware of this. As I went through the very difficult process of facing my traumas, my insecurities, my shortcomings, and even my self-esteem or self-worth, I realized that I was stronger than I thought I was.

But this strong was different.

You see, in the past, through all of the different challenges and difficulties that I faced, I came to a place where I had put up walls and really kind of hardened my outside to protect the soft inside. You know, it's interesting. My zodiac sign is Cancer, which is symbolized by a crab. As you know, a crab has a hard exoskeleton. It has a hard shell on the outside, but when you crack through that hard shell, it's nothing but soft tissue on the inside. That's really how I've gone through much of my life: like that crab, with the hard shell on the outside, daring anyone to penetrate it to get to the best part – the soft meat on the inside.

Here's another analogy for you. Let's say you're using your hands to shovel in your garden. You're digging the shovel into the ground and lifting out the earth. You're doing that process repeatedly for hours. That repetitive motion throughout the day causes calluses to develop on your hands. The calluses are formed because of continual irritation to the skin from the repetitive action. It is your body's way of defending the more vulnerable muscle tissue below the skin from harm. It's your body's defense against injury. It's your body's defense against irritation. If you repeat that process over and over and over again, those callouses can become so hard and large, and it can take concentrated effort to remove the buildup.

Our hearts are the same way. When we are continually placed in situations and circumstances that hurt us, irritate us, and cause us pain and injury, it can cause callouses to form on our emotional heart. The heart is a muscle. It is soft tissue, but over time, from repeated injury, it can harden and become emotionally calloused. It requires intentional effort to heal and remove all of those callouses from our heart. I'm using this metaphorically, but that buildup is all of our past hurt. It's heartbreak. It's disappointment. It's anger. It's betrayal. It's all those things that others have done which have brought us pain and caused us to put up another layer of protection around ourselves.

After the breakup with my new love interest, I allowed myself to feel all of the pain, all the disappointment, all the heartache from not just this situation but every unhealed situation that I had swept under the rug over my entire life. Because, let's be honest, rarely do we actually sit with our emotions. We might tolerate them for a moment. We might have a good cry, but then we pick ourselves up and move on. We take the stance that "I'm not going to allow anyone else to hurt me in that way ever again." We don't allow ourselves to actually heal. We just push it down, adding another layer to the callous.

My entire life, that's what I did until now. I finally allowed myself the space to actually feel everything. It wasn't easy. There were many days when I didn't know if I could do it. I wanted to escape, but I was so deep in the process that I had no choice but to go through to the other side. And in the depths of my despair, I came to realize that it is not my responsibility to protect my heart from others.

I'm not saying just be out here willy-nilly with your heart or not be cautious. It is still important to use wisdom. People are responsible for their own actions. It is not our responsibility to make them "treat us right." I think as women, we tend to allow people to do things we don't like, that hurt us or that bring us pain and discomfort. Because we're nurturers, we will forgive them and continue to maintain relationships with them. I'm not just referring to romantic relationships, but friendships, professional relationships, associations, even familial relationships.

When we do that, we are teaching them how to treat us. We are teaching them what we will accept. Honestly, we should not be surprised when we get more of the same. If we can really understand that, it becomes easy for us to remain soft and open rather than closed off. But to do that requires strength. It's like walking around as a crab without an exoskeleton, without the outer hard shell. We're much more likely to get hurt, to get bruised, to be injured without that protection.

However, if we can do that, people get to experience the best part of us. They don't have to fight to get to the good stuff. If you can allow yourself to be open, to be soft, to be available, recognizing that, yes, you're going to get a little bruised, you might get a little bump; you might get tossed around a little. But in doing that, it's easier for you to recognize when someone is not good for you. If you've got your hard shell on or if you've got your walls up, then those first few blows, you're not actually going to feel. They have to break through the wall before they can even get to the soft part. Then once you've finally allowed them in, it's going to hurt so much more. So if you could allow yourself to stay open, at the very first sign of inconsistency, at the very first sign of them not being a good fit for your life, it will be so much easier for you to walk away.

My encouragement to you is to take some time if you need it. Take some time to go inward. Allow yourself to feel all the feels, no matter how uncomfortable it is, so that you can heal. When you emerge, you can emerge without that hardness. You'll come out with the strength of the softness so that you give the world only the best part of you. Then the world gets to determine how much of you they get in their lives based on how they interact with you. Because now at the first sign of anything that is harmful, you'll be able to recognize it and take appropriate action.

"We need women who are so strong they can be gentle, so educated they can be humble, so fierce they can be compassionate, so passionate they can be rational, and so disciplined they can be free."

—Kavita Ramdas

Tamara A. Baldwin is an international bestselling author, minister, educator, and academic advocate for underserved populations, including alternative, special-needs, first generation graduates and juvenile offenders. Tamara is a transformational coach and demonstrates her life purpose of encouraging, empowering, and equipping those whom she encounters to live with purpose and intentionality.

Personally, and professionally, Tamara has positively impacted innumerable lives and holds a master's degree in Ministry Leadership. With her second master's degree she will serve as a Licensed Professional Clinical Mental Health Counselor, specializing in restoration counseling for anxiety, depression, trauma, religious and spiritual abuse recovery.

Tamara is honored God chose her to birth her now priceless adult son, Anthony, who inspires her to write. Tamara seeks to share her life experiences as a testimony of God's truth in action and believes that we sow into the kingdom of God by serving his people, which takes undeniable strength that comes from God, and God alone.

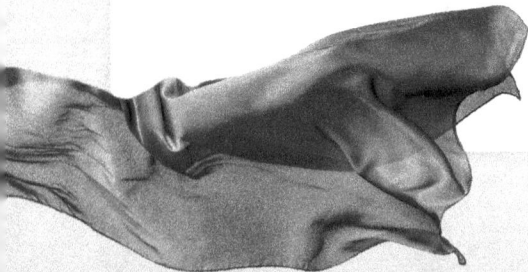

Enduring the Race
by God's Grace

Tamara Baldwin

"He gives power to the faint, and to him who has no might he increases strength. Even youths shall faint, and be weary, and young men shall fall exhausted; but they who wait for the Lord shall renew their strength; they shall mount up with wings like eagles; they shall run and not be weary; they shall walk and not faint" (Isaiah 40: 29-31, ESV).

It has been said that a strong woman fears nothing, but a woman of strength shows courage when subjected to fearful situations. As I think about this statement I am reminded of the countless times since childhood that I was expected to exemplify strength, obedience, and leadership. As a child I was expected to hold my head up high regardless of the circumstances or situations around me. My parents expected nothing less than excellence, even though I was a child.

Now, as an adult, I attribute the firm teaching, the discipline, and the expectation to live a life that pleases God and serves Him as God's hand extended as a gift. Since childhood I have been afforded a gift and an opportunity to live the word of God, not just speak of the word. The undeniable strength of a woman comes in the form of having God at the forefront and the center of everything that I do. There have also been times along the journey when I have been questioned as to how I cope, function, manage, and maintain sanity and composure while experiencing countless traumatic situations and circumstances. Sometimes the question has been rhetorical and yet other times the one inquiring earnestly seeks a response, and I undoubtedly attribute my triumph to undeniable strength obtained by God.

One of the most challenging tasks to complete, whether at home, work, place of worship, or in the community, is the audacious task of explaining where one's strength comes from, yet since childhood, I have been trained to live my life in the way of the Lord. As I reflect on the undeniable strength of God, the first death I can remember was the death of my paternal grandmother when I was three. The feelings I remember were not yet formed, as I was so young; therefore, I do not recall the exact feelings I had at the time. This was, however, the first wake I attended, and I did not attend the funeral service. The thing I remember most, regardless of my age, was an expectation to conduct myself in a manner that was poised, polite, and quiet.

To draw attention to myself was unacceptable, funeral or otherwise. Even as a child, God's strength was shaping me to eventually endure a day that is forever etched in my memory and on my heart: the death of my mother, who was a trailblazing, brilliant, artistic, yet underestimated and undervalued daughter, sister, friend, wife, and mother of four fraternal twin girls and two younger boys, professional musician, licensed and ordained minister of the gospel of Christ Jesus, who experienced a heart attack and unexpectedly passed away in accordance with God's calendar and timing.

It was God's strength that sustained me during this time, as I was just weeks away from obtaining my Master's degree in ministry leadership. Final projects were assigned and although unspeakably challenging, it was the Holy Spirit that sustained my mind, heart, and soul with strength to complete course requirements. This experience became a teachable moment as it relates to death, dying and loss. Through this time of unfamiliar gut-wrenching pain, anguish, and despair, I was reminded that life obstacles do not cancel our God assignments. Therefore, I coped with this loss having pride as my mother's firstborn child.

I coped with this loss and even recalled Mother making the statement: "If I could have chosen a daughter on my own, I would have chosen you." This was the most difficult death for me, in that there was still so much I needed to glean from my mother. God's undeniable strength was the foundation that kept me, especially when needing to be strong for my only child, whose bond with my mother was far beyond that which I could have ever thought or imagined.

Because both my son and my mother are musicians, their Nana (grandmother) and grandson conversations would continue for hours, into the night and morning, as they mused over musical techniques, chord progressions and melodies which sacredly minted their hearts as one. Interestingly, at the time of my mother's demise, we were learning about each other from a new perspective. I was learning mother through the lens of a mother, and Mother was learning about me as an adult rather than a little girl.

As it relates to my son being an only child, it is my desire that he takes the opportunity afforded to know me rather than just what he perceives about me. I am convinced that God offers an indescribable and undeniable strength for the journey that takes place between children and their parents. Both parent and child learn the significance, importance, and value of authenticity as well as openness throughout the process. As I think about the strength needed to cope with loss and acceptance of God's will concerning my life, I know my grief is resolved when instead of presenting a hopeless and helpless demeanor, I consider God's word that states: "Fear not, for I am with you, be not dismayed, for I am your God. I will strengthen you. I will help you. I will uphold you with my righteous hand" (Isaiah 41:10, English Standard Version).

God's undeniable strength has been evident in all significant areas of my life.

When God speaks, it strengthens those who heed his word. During this time, one becomes committed in a greater way and makes a choice to allow God's word to manifest through action. Further, my strengthened commitment to Christ includes a daily and necessary action plan of prayer, offering gratitude and thanksgiving, seeking guidance and direction from the Holy Spirit, meditation on the word of God, reading the word of God, reflective journaling, as well as praise and worship. I am reminded of the numerous ways in which God has been a consistent, faithful, loving, forgiving refuge and strength. I am both proud and certain that I am by divine design selected, chosen, and positioned as a leader. Some suggest leaders are made rather than born, yet I am proof that it takes undeniable strength to be both.

My current commitment to Christ is the result of innumerable and significant factors from age eleven, when I accepted Christ into my heart, to present. The journey has been a gift and is one whereby my walk, talk, and thoughts are attributed to both a God-ordained and spirit-led life mandate to serve as God's hand extended. I do believe God endowed me with strength to journey through ministry experiences that have been life changing. Since before accepting Christ as my Lord and Savior, I recall being told that I was wise and discerning far beyond my years. Interestingly, I also recall with great clarity the opportunity to shadow and eventually teach Sunday school beginning at age 14.

It was during this experience that God gave me strength to be mentored and groomed to share the good news of Jesus. Although I was young, I learned what it meant to be sanctified and set apart for the work of the ministry. Thus my ministry experience has been an ongoing progression toward my God-ordained destiny.

Throughout my young adult years to present, I have experienced a whirlwind of teachable moments where I found strength that has primed, pruned, and prepared me for my journey, which results in me developing a unique lens from which I view ministry.

Because of God's strength bestowed on me, I have served in various congregations and denominations in many areas and roles: Minister of Music, Director of Christian Education, Associate Pastor, Workplace Chaplain, Pastoral Care Leader, Vocational Rehabilitation Counselor, and ongoing participation in general church ministries. With gratitude I recognize that my ministry experience continues to serve as a transformative testimony of God's truth in action. According to Philippians 4:19: "My God will supply all of my needs according to His riches in glory by Christ Jesus." Looking back, I realize God gave me strength as a child to befriend those who were different, ostracized, bullied, or just did not seem to fit in.

These individuals were drawn to me, which compelled me to have a genuine concern for the comfort, wellbeing, and equitable treatment of someone other than myself. Not surprisingly, countless memories saturate my mind regarding God's strength as it relates to family and friends who have affirmed what I believe to be strength and divine ability to discern, defuse, empathize, and connect with those who are hurt, hurting, down, depressed, helpless, hopeless or who simply need guidance and support. Many times, when we encounter the above circumstances, our thoughts are not focused on God's strength, but how long the struggle will last, and how we can be done sooner rather than later.

It is not until we are on the other side of what we have endured that we realize how we made it through. God's word in Isaiah 40:31 says: "But they that wait upon the Lord shall renew their strength; they shall mount up with wings as eagles; they shall run, and not be weary; and they shall walk, and not faint."

I am grateful for God's strength to serve his people, regardless of their circumstances. Through the process I have learned that our identity in Christ is where we find not only peace but undeniable strength. Further, it is through God's strength that we are offered an opportunity to recognize who we are and who he created us to be. God's word says, "I will guide you along the best pathway for your life. I will advise you and watch over you" (Psalm 32:8, New Living Translation). God specifically and explicitly assures us that we are never alone. We do not have to guess, wonder, and surmise because He has been, is, and will always be with us. I am reminded of moments along my journey where, because of my upbringing, I continuously love, give, forgive, adjust, sacrifice, compromise, pivot, and shift, but only by God's strength.

In fact, it is this strength for which I am known. I am a friend who, for since I can remember, has always been trustworthy, honest, non-judgmental, and accommodating, typically leaving an encounter or the presence of others totally depleted rather than fueled. Indeed, I have been jolted into the reality that I am admittedly more of a friend to individuals I perceived as friends but who otherwise seek to use me for what I share freely. My nature is not to perceive being used as much as it is feeling honored to be thought of to meet a need, ultimately bringing God glory.

Undoubtedly, it is God's strength that allows me to push past what others perceive as being used and taken for granted as an opportunity to serve as God's hand extended in the world. "Be strong in the Lord and in the power of his might" (Ephesians 6:10, King James Version). In this regard, we are wise to become equipped with necessary tools to use that will foster healing for those who are hurting or who remain in a time warp from either emotional or psychological trauma.

Not surprisingly, our interaction with others, as well as how we perceive the world, is directly connected to how we navigate through life experiences, good or bad. Just as it takes strength to focus on nutrition, fitness, supplements, and equipment to maintain our health, it takes strength to act by God's leading rather than our own flesh. "My flesh and my heart faileth: but God is the strength of my heart, and my portion forever" (Psalm 73:26, English Standard Version). How often do we consider how our thoughts affect our actions?

Regardless of life challenges, struggles, obstacles, setbacks, and circumstances far beyond our control, obstacles do not cancel our life assignments. And only by God's strength are we transformed. God's strength is made perfect in our weakness. It has been said that our greatest treasure on earth is our identity in Christ. When we know who we are, we are better able and equipped to function the way God intended. Establishing a strong identity is important; much like our identity in Christ, we must know who we are to represent the kingdom of God well.

Another reason for a strong identity has to do with our personal values. Interestingly, it is necessary to acknowledge my personal identity along the way. Quite perplexing is how one so steeped in culture, social protocol, and etiquette could, as an adult, be so bound by so many debilitating life challenges. Yet, through strength that comes from God, I feel a liberating need to dig deeper, moving beyond the periphery of distractions, obstacles, self-doubt, and debilitating stress that has surfaced toward liberating freedom from barriers of the past.

The process of pushing past the surface has been therapeutic and has further confirmed not only that I was created in the image of God, but that God has ordained my life to impact change. "And I am sure of this, that he who began a good work in you will bring it to completion at the day of Jesus Christ" (Philippians. 1:6, New Living Translation).

During times in my life when I have been hurt and troubled by doing for others, giving to others, and exhausting myself to please others without receiving anything in return, God gave me strength to earnestly pray for those with whom I had an authentic relationship, until finally realizing I had fallen prey to countless situation-ships. Naturally, after wallowing in self-pity, resentment, and questions of "Why is this happening to me?" or "Why are things not happening for me?" my mind was overhauled by the strength of God's word and my thinking became clear, in that I must adhere to God's word in (Romans 12:1-2, New International Version): "Therefore, I urge you, brothers and sisters, in view of God's mercy, to offer your bodies as a living sacrifice, holy and pleasing to God—this is your true and proper worship. Do not conform to the pattern of this world but be transformed by the renewing of your mind."

Oh, how grateful I am to be stronger than the paralyzing opinions of other people. Finally, I am stronger than the self-sabotaging bondage of a mindset of mediocrity. Although challenging, my decision to embrace God's strength has further been liberating and has served as a catalyst for positive change, resulting in a healed heart made stronger by my relationship with God. Strong relationships must be nurtured daily, and our relationship with God is no different. Moreover, fostering and maintaining a relationship with God is the most important. Whether through reading the word of God, praying, meditating, worshipping, or serving others, we must endeavor to acknowledge and recognize the countless moments of our lives where God has, is and continues to strengthen us as we live a life that is holy, pleasing, and acceptable to him.

When we are weak, we must depend on God, who gives us strength. When we read and meditate, we must depend on God, who gives us strength. When we seek God's will for our lives through prayer, we must depend on God, who gives us strength. When we trust and obey God's word, we must depend on God, who gives us strength. When we worship God in spirit and in truth, we must depend on God, who gives us strength. When we assemble ourselves with other believers, we must depend on God, who gives us strength. When we allow the movement of the Holy Spirit to empower us, we must depend on God, who gives us strength. Our very existence depends on God and the strength he breathes on and through us to endure that which comes our way.

You too can develop undeniable strength by accepting God's promise that he will never leave nor forsake his own. Our steadfast faith in God is the foundation of what it means to live with humility, integrity, and authenticity. The undeniable strength of a woman is gifted to a woman whose life experiences serve as either seeds or fertilizer for those who existed before us, or who will exist once we exist no longer. Our strength as women is an ongoing process of development in a garden of femininity and grace. In this regard we must acknowledge and recognize that simply being a female does not equate to being a lady or woman of dignity and unwavering character.

Finding strength to share my own experiences surfaces from acknowledging that self-disclosure occurs when it is beneficial for others seeking encouragement and insight. As a woman, I believe my history of loss and grief will positively impact those whom I serve. In this regard, I know beyond a doubt that what others perceive as strength in me is undoubtedly the undeniable strength of God, who directs my path both personally and professionally. "Be strong and of good courage, do not fear nor be afraid of them; for the Lord your God, He is the One who goes with you. He will not leave you nor forsake you" (Deuteronomy 31:6, New International Version). God is our refuge and strength. God has strategically designed your life purpose. The undeniable strength of a woman is a gift from God. Embrace it, respect it, protect it, and treasure it. You are a mighty workmanship of God's Undeniable Strength.

Jerri St. John is the owner of JewelsfromJerri, LLC and resides in Maryland, USA. She is an empty-nester, wife, mother and grandmother. Jerri has been on her own since the age of sixteen. Having experienced many challenges throughout her life, including the challenges of depression, morbid obesity, childhood abuse, and domestic violence, she has turned her life around to help other women who struggle with similar issues. Her life's passion and purpose are inspiring and encouraging other women to find their inner strength and beauty; becoming the best version of themselves possible.

Jerri is a Certified Life Coach, Master Coach, Best-Selling Author, Public Speaker, Podcast Host, and Independent Stylist with Color Street. She strives to be a light in the world; spreading joy, hope and positivity. Jerri considers her strong faith, optimism, love of people and her positive outlook to be her greatest strengths. Reach Jerri through her website: https://jewelsfromjerri.net

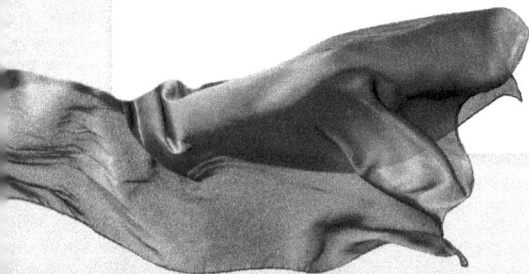

Kissing Frogs:
A Love Story

Jerri St. John

I grew up in an era of Disney princesses, "Happily Ever After" and preparing oneself to meet the right man, who would sweep me off my feet and make my life a dream come true. This is the goal that most girls aspired to at the time. It didn't matter how smart you were or whatever else an individual might want to do with their life. When a girl found her "prince" – she was fulfilled.

Unfortunately, that was not the reality that life handed me. I grew up in a household that was not only dysfunctional, but also abusive, neglectful and downright toxic. With a father who was either completely physically absent, emotionally absent or abusive when he WAS around, I spent most of my life seeking male attention, approval and love. It was something that was deep inside my subconscious and caused me to make choices throughout my life that could have destroyed me (and did for a time). I ultimately developed into a strong, independent woman who stopped allowing the "frogs" to get the best of her. I use the term "frogs" because I not only had to kiss a lot of them before finding my prince – I also MARRIED them!

So – no judgment here because I've judged, criticized, hated myself and lived with guilt, shame and blame for more years than not.

SO – WHO WERE THOSE FROGS?

Frog #1:

He was my high school sweetheart. I met him through a mutual cousin on opposite sides of the family. He was edgy, good look-ing, a bad boy of sorts. We flirted and fell for each other very quickly, getting engaged when I graduated high school. He was a serial cheater, liar, drug abuser and someone who took away my youth, my innocence and my trust. We married after I had left him and returned from New Jersey to California. He came searching for me after I had started college, joined a sorority and was dating other people. He convinced me that he still loved me, that he had changed and that we deserved a second chance. We got married and I don't even remember where or how, but I returned with him to New Jersey for a short time and wound up escaping with the shirt on my back and a few belongings to get away from him. I stayed with relatives for a while, until I was able to get my own apartment and live on my own.

Frog #2:

We met at a fraternity party. He was flirty, gorgeous and friendly. I fell hard. He lived about 200 miles away so we saw each other as we were able and decided that I would move in with him. It was a constant party and we always had other people in our home. There were red flags all over the place, with keg parties and drugs being abundant in our lives. I married him anyway, stayed with him for 6-1/2 years, had a son with him and also continued my descent into self-loathing and shame. He was an alcoholic and drug abuser who took no responsibility for anything in his life. It was a struggle being married to someone whose mistress was a six-pack of beer and a joint. Again, I left with nearly nothing, even though I had built up our life by buying a home and was the main breadwinner. He couldn't hold a job, having thirteen jobs in the 6-1/2 years we were together. His form of abuse was being emotionally unavailable and refusing to take any responsibility. I was no longer FUN because I became an adult and took responsibility for a home and a child.

Frog #3:

I met him through a dating site and he presented himself as a successful businessman, father and upstanding citizen. I was barely getting by financially, with no support system, a toddler, a full-time job, and had just come off a nasty divorce. I moved in with him very quickly because of my desperation for stability and a roof over my head. I walked into a situation of being a maid, sex object, and surrogate mother to his two little girls. He abused my son and encouraged me to do the same. He was regularly taking all sorts of drugs and drinking way too much. He had perverse appetites and disgusting habits as well as a violent and depressed streak. I got my son out of the house and moved him in with his father and grandmother. I feared for my life after I walked in on him with a rifle pointed down his throat. That frightened me so badly that I ran away with nothing but the clothes on my back and a few personal items yet again. I escaped back to Southern California to the security of friends who temporarily provided me with housing until I could get back on my feet. I was able to get a good job and my own apartment fairly quickly, but I found myself traumatized and at a very low point once again.

Frog #4:

We met on the driving range after I took up golf. We talked, we flirted, I met his mother. He was awkward and there was nothing flashy or exciting about him. He paid attention to me. We had some fun. Again, living alone in an apartment, struggling to get by financially, when he asked me to move in with him and later to marry him, I agreed, even though the red flags were all there. This one wasn't an alcoholic or a drug abuser, but he WAS extremely mentally abusive. He reminded me of my parents, constantly tearing me down, criticizing me and beating me down emotionally.

It was the spring of 1991. I had been living with mental abuse for almost two years. One day, I just snapped and couldn't take it anymore. I was constantly being told how fat I was, even though I was at a healthy weight. Nothing I did was good enough and even though this FROG made a good living and provided for many of my needs, I couldn't stand being around him. Even my vacuuming capabilities were called into question as he insisted on doing everything over again because he could see lines and they weren't straight. I had a meltdown and realized one day that I just would not tolerate one more night in his bed. I immediately moved myself into the guest room. The ultimate goal was to get a job and get back on my feet after dabbling in self-employment for a couple of years.

I bought myself a computer to automate some of my business inventory and discovered the world of Bulletin Board Services, with access to the outside world. I had been feeling very isolated and alone with FROG #4. I was a social butterfly whose wings had not only been clipped, but completely chopped off. I needed to grow them back.

As I crawled and clawed my way to competency with the computer, I had support from a friend who was a computer consultant. He and his wife were self-employed and he made sure I had everything I needed to get the computer integrated into my business. The computer opened up a whole new world of "friends" to chat with, which helped alleviate some of my loneliness and lack of self-esteem.

I was through with men! FROG #4 had controlled me, mentally beat me down and isolated me from my family and friends. This relationship also opened my eyes to the fact that if I didn't change something about the people I was attracting into my life, I was doomed to continue making the same mistakes. I was mentally and physically drained, always trying to live up to others' expectations of who I should be and how I should act. I was at my lowest point and decided that if I was a failure at romantic relationships, then I probably didn't deserve to have one.

I threw myself into networking, working my business, and self-improvement. I spent evenings alone in the guest room, chatting with anonymous, faceless people behind the computer screen. What I found there was a bit terrifying: men who wanted to get together for drinks and sex. Definitely NOT what I was seeking. I made sure to keep my identity and location private and started getting sick feelings in my stomach from this virtual "meat market" that was the world of BBS (Bulletin Board Services.)

Just as I was contemplating the idea of cancelling these services, I received a message from someone clear across the country. It was friendly and chatty and extremely innocuous. I responded back and we struck up a conversation that nearly ended when he sent me a digital rose and, as a computer newbie, I interpreted it as something inappropriate and sexual. When he explained what it was (after I told him I was uncomfortable), we had a great laugh and became fast friends.

The anonymity of the computer in the days before the Internet was a safe haven for us to divulge all of our secrets, let down our guards, and get to know each other on a deep level. I was NOT looking for any sort of relationship and made that very clear. I felt he was SAFE. He lived 3,000 miles away and was twelve years younger than me, yet we connected so completely over a month of chatting daily. We talked about our failed relationships, lives, goals, dreams and our histories.

Our computer chats were limited by the time difference and time constraints, as the service limited us to an hour a day. Eventually that hour wasn't enough time for us and we graduated to phone calls. I'll never forget the first time I heard his voice with the thick New Jersey accent. We talked and talked for hours on end about anything and everything. I had never connected with another human being at this level in my entire life and yet I was leery. I was cautious and afraid.

"What if you're an axe murderer?" He wasn't.

"What if I'm 300 pounds?" I wasn't.

None of that mattered. Our friendship continued to blossom into something more solid. This man accepted me for who I was, with no judgment or criticism. It seemed too good to be true. It no longer scared me, but I was hesitant to believe it could ever be anything more than long distance friendship.

After running up phone bills that were larger than either of our monthly rents, we decided we needed to meet in person. We had exchanged pictures by mail and he was not the type of guy I ever would have given a second look. He wasn't slick, showy or a "bad boy" type. He was a BABY. What on earth was I doing? What was I thinking? I was falling in love with this guy and who he was rather than jumping into bed with someone and mistaking it for love. I was still hesitant, constantly waiting for the other shoe to drop, because I didn't trust myself to make good decisions in the romance department. Just LOOK at my track record! I just had to find out if this was real, so I started making plans to visit him in Maryland.

My friends tried to talk me out of it. They truly believed I had lost my mind. "Why are you traveling 3,000 miles to meet him? If he cares about you as much as he says, then he should come out here." I heard and respected all of the reasons why I SHOULDN'T go, but I needed to do this for ME. What was the worst thing that could happen?

It bothered me that I was jumping from one relationship to another so soon, but I had been separated emotionally and physically from FROG #4 for quite a while. Even though I was living in his home, we never saw or spoke to each other.

I was both excited and terrified during the entire airplane ride across country. I questioned everything about my seemingly impulsive decision to drop everything and travel to Maryland. All of my doubts melted away as we spotted each other in airport terminal. He scooped me up in his arms and we held each other tightly as we kissed for the first time. We had bonded and knew each other better than most people who've lived together for years. I knew then that I had made the right decision.

We spent two weeks exploring, making plans and falling in love. We were connected in a way that still blows my mind to this day. We could read each other's' minds, finish each other's sentences and knew instinctively what each other needed. It was meant to be and I believe that when I surrendered and "gave up," God brought this amazing man into my life. He was the first person in my life, besides my grandmother, who completely accepted me for who I am and loved me unconditionally.

We had long conversations about the implications of our age difference. It concerned me. It didn't bother him at all. He was an "old soul" who acted and looked more mature than his chronological age. I was a child whose growth had been stunted by childhood trauma that carried into my adult life, so we were essentially the same age.

I went back to California after that two-week visit, packed up my belongings, and made plans to move to Maryland and my new life a month later. To say that I was confident and sure of what I was doing would be a lie. I was completely terrified, yet hopeful. We had discussed our values, ideas and everything important while we were together, but I had an underlying distrust and insecurity about men because of my past. Men had always betrayed me and yet I felt that this was an opportunity to change the narrative of my life.

We adjusted to living together very easily and went through a honeymoon phase of enjoying each other and having fun. Then I settled in, got a job, made a few friends and started creating a life in Maryland. The difference in this relationship was the love and respect that we had for each other. We listened and encouraged each other and continue to do that to this day.

Over our thirty-one years together we have never had a fight. People don't believe us when we tell them that we don't argue. We've always believed it's because we didn't want drama in our lives and had both already been through terrible relationships. We knew what we didn't want from a relationship and we were committed to not repeating those mistakes. The key to our success has been the fact that we always communicate with each other and listen to each other. We had a lot of hurdles to overcome in those early days, but we knew we would get through them together.

One of the hurdles was that we were both still legally married to other people. We filed for divorces and waited for them to become final so that we could get married. It took a year, and we got married as soon as we were legally able. We improved our financial situation with better jobs, better living space and continued personal growth with a forward momentum that has continued throughout our years together.

I had a past that was full of pain and failed relationships. I had suffered abuse and neglect from the time I was small and he nurtured me, and provided me with a safe space to grow and learn to trust.

So much had changed with this unconditional love in my life. We had solidified our relationship, joined a church community and immersed ourselves in the life of the church. We became youth leaders even though neither of us had experience with pre-teens and teens. Neither one of us had a strong faith background and it was something that became very important to us as we grew as a couple and eventually as a family.

Eventually I started wanting to be a parent with this man. I had failed miserably with my biological son and it still breaks my heart that I didn't provide him with the parenting he deserved. I never had role models or support to learn how to be a parent. Being married to FROG #2, a practicing alcoholic and drug abuser, made it extremely complicated. I had made the decision to have my tubes tied several years after divorcing FROG #2 because I didn't believe I deserved to be a parent after the disaster that was my first parenting experience. Finding love, acceptance and realizing my own value changed many things. The burning desire to share this love with a child, to become a parent was haunting me and we decided to look into the possibility of expanding our family. In 1995 we adopted our daughter, at the age of 6-1/2, and we have been able to experience the love and joy of being parents.

That year, I was also diagnosed with clinical depression. It was severe and changed my entire personality. I received treatment and still struggled to find myself inside the pain and anger of the depression. This was the only time that I was in fear of losing the one person who meant everything in the world to me.

I'll never forget the night that the fear of losing him slapped me across the face and finally started me on the road to healing from the depression. We were at a Bruce Springsteen concert and instead of having a good time, holding hands and cuddling up, he was distant and cold. I had never seen this side of him before and I was in tears most of the night. We drove home in silence and when we pulled up in our driveway, we had a heart-to-heart talk about his feelings of loss and helplessness with my depression. This disease had almost succeeded in tearing us apart, but it was the turning point that eventually built back our trust and made us stronger than ever before. When he saw how hurt I was and that I didn't want him to leave, we had a starting point from which we could start rebuilding. That was the closest thing to an argument and yet it wasn't even an argument. It was a turning point. Up until that point, he didn't see any other options than to split up. I fought hard to save my marriage that night and opened up about my love for him, my fears, my self-loathing, my insecurities – baring my soul. I vowed to get better, find a solution to this horrible darkness, and begged him to stay. The thought of losing this amazing man who had come into my life terrified me.

He knew it was the disease causing these changes in me, but he felt helpless against the disease and didn't see any other solution. Thankfully our love and commitment to each other won out and we were able to build back stronger and better than ever. I promised I'd find a solution and I did.

For years, I was so ashamed of my history with men and all of my failed relationships, that I kept the secret and would only talk about being "divorced" but never discuss how many times. I realized one day that all of these experiences are part of what made me who I am today and even though I walked away from each one of these relationships, I was NOT a failure! Instead, I reframed my thinking and realized that I was a survivor. I was strong, courageous and brave to finally choose my own well-being above that of the "security" of a marriage or a relationship. Without these experiences, I wouldn't be the confident, happy woman that I am today. We have to overcome (and even embrace) the challenges in life to be able to appreciate the blessings.

I wake up every single day with the gratitude and knowledge that my life could have turned out much differently. I could have been a drug addict, a prostitute or, even worse, dead way before my time. God was protecting me and looking out for me and second, the unconditional love of a wonderful man allowed me the freedom to grow, to heal, and to become the woman who was begging to blossom and reveal herself.

It's said that one has to kiss a lot of frogs before they find their prince. I definitely kissed AND married more than my share of frogs in search of my prince, my forever love, the person who accepts and loves me unconditionally, who helped me to see that I deserved much better from my life. He is the only person I can be with 24/7, 365 and never get tired of being together. He is MY person—the one who makes me laugh, supports me and GETS me! We've been together for almost 31 years. It only gets better and stronger with time. We never run out of things to talk about, laugh about or share. We have total love and respect for each other. I dreamt for many, many years of finding this kind of love but never believed it was possible for me. He has helped me to grow and finally become the confident, self-assured, bad-ass woman that I am today! SO if you're keeping track, yes, this is my FIFTH marriage and I'm grateful that I never have to kiss another frog in my life!

Thank you, Jonathan St. John!!!

This is a love story... a tribute to the amazing love and beautiful life that we created together. You are everything to me and even though I kissed all of those frogs, they were the appetizer that made me appreciate the full course meal that would be our life together. I can't wait to see what our next chapter brings.

Monique Johnson is a Special Educator, Licensed Massage Therapist, and a Published Author. She is a highly respected professional in her community.

Ms. Johnson, a veteran Special Education Teacher with Baltimore City Public Schools, has provided over 28 years of dedicated service to children and their families. Currently, Ms. Johnson provides specialized instruction to children with special needs, in which many of them have Autism. She lends behavioral and academic support to families of special needs children.

Education is not Ms. Johnson's only passion and accomplishment, entrepreneurship is prevalent, alongside her career in education. Taking inspiration from her maternal grandmother, who suffered from Arthritis and Dementia, Monique completed coursework at the Baltimore School of Massage. She is a Licensed Massage Therapist in the state of Maryland and is the proud owner of Lavender Dreams Mobile Spa.

Writing has become integral and steadfast in Ms. Johnson's life. She is a Contributing Author in the Amazon #1 Bestseller, Queens Who Defied the Odds: Resiliency Is Not Just Surviving but Thriving.

Monique is a native New Yorker from St. Albans, Queens. Currently, she resides in Windsor Mill, Maryland.

Email: monique.johnson5556@gmail.com
Website: lavenderdreamsmobilespa.com
Website: moniquejohnsonwrites.com
Email: moniquejohnsonwrites@gmail.com

Sleeping with the Enemy

Monique Johnson

Foggy Haze

Foggy Haze

> Sitting in a daze,
> Going through the motions for days,
> Not sure, feeling insecure,
> Questioning and second-guessing self.
> Anxiety creeps in;
> Fear follows

Foggy Haze

> Sitting in a daze,
> Feeling confused,
> Feeling bewildered,
> Feeling like you're losing your state of mind.

Foggy Haze

> Sitting in a daze,
> Feeling drained,
> Feeling insane,
> Feeling broken,
> Feeling inhumane.

Foggy Haze
>Sitting in a daze,
>Chasing false hope like its dope,
>Enslaved by the mask.

GOD HELP ME…TAKE IT AWAY…NOW…

Domestic violence has become prevalent and is the leading cause of injury to women, according to domesticviolencestatistics.org. The statistics are startling. Domestic violence is real, and we may have loved ones experiencing this, or perhaps the reader has experienced some form of domestic violence in their lifetime.

Domestic violence has many faces. It's not always physical violence, according to the AZ Coalition to End Sexual and Domestic Violence (www.acesdv.org). Domestic violence is any behavior the purpose of which is to gain power and control over a spouse, partner, girl/boyfriend or intimate family member. Abuse is a learned behavior; it is not caused by anger, mental problems, drugs or alcohol, or other common excuses. There are multiple types of abuse: Control, Physical Abuse, Sexual Abuse, Emotional Abuse & Intimidation, Isolation, Verbal Abuse: Coercion, Threats, & Blame, Using Male Privilege, and Economic Abuse.

Domestic violence knocked on my door. I would witness or hear stories of other women getting mistreated. However, I never thought in my wildest dreams that I would experience some form of domestic violence. I've experienced domestic violence through dating and a relationship. My story will focus on the long-term relationship that I was engaged in.

My Story

Boy oh boy, this man is quite the charmer! Everyone seems to fondly know him. He is aesthetically pleasing to the eye with his smooth, rich skin. His eyes crinkle and twinkle, as his smile widens from ear to ear. This man walks with an easygoing, proud stride, and stands with a strong, confident posture. When he talks, it sounds like a song. The words flow with ease, as he often tells a story. He always had a story to tell! However, there's a deep-rooted dark energy that surfaces and causes havoc. Early on, the red flags were shining brightly directly in my face. The thought of "potential" overlooked all red flags and became dormant. Now, something that is dormant will resurface again, in due time. It didn't take long for those red flags to rear their ugly heads, after being dormant.

The Beginning

It was innocent in the beginning. As I look back, I believe that I was purposely preyed upon.

We met at school and were attending the same classes. During our first day of classes, he stood out from the crowd. When responding to questions, he would confidently answer, and asked questions too. He was easygoing and charmed staff and students with his humor and direct approach. We were friendly toward each other and worked closely on group class activities.

Classes had us quite busy and were intense. Many of us worked full-time jobs during the day and spent our evenings during the week for class. We spent a lot of time together, and many of us had formed our tribes, our study buddies.

During this time, I was single and not looking for love. The focus was to complete coursework for my trade license. Romantic relationships were far from my mind...not even on my radar. However, as time went on, a shift began to happen.

Michael and I spent more and more time together. We began to sit together with our tribe every night. Our tribe was awesome! We supported each other through class sessions during and after school. Outside of school, together, we would tighten our notes, do homework, and study for quizzes and exams. This tribe was the start of newfound friendships. It felt so right and natural to me. I became comfortable and allowed my guard to fall. Boy oh boy, as soon as I let my guard down, Michael began to swoop in.

Michael and I became familiar and comfortable around each other in our group. We became so comfortable that one evening, Michael decided to initiate more conversation alone, away from our tribe. Honestly, I feel that this was the beginning of being preyed upon. One night, as the class was preparing for a dinner break, I had left the group to use the restroom. Well, guess who was waiting nearby. It was Michael casually standing alone, as if he was waiting for someone. Mhmmm, that someone was me. At the time, I didn't think anything out of the ordinary. As I embarked up the hallway, Michael got my attention and stated, "Do you know that you have an aura about you?" I'm looking at him, like, "What?" I'm thinking to myself, *What is he saying?* Michael must have read my mind because he proceeded to tell me that I had such a bright light illuminating from my body, particularly around my head. "Oh really," I said, just smiling back at him. We continued to casually talk. He was such a good-looking man—tall, dark, and handsome. When he talked, it sounded like he was singing.

Michael and I began our whirlwind of a ride. He was charming and interesting to talk to. We began to talk regularly during and after class. Let the "love-bombing" begin! He would bring me food for dinner and always had a story to tell. Endless compliments. Little did I know that I was being preyed upon. During that time, I was in a vulnerable state. Work was stressful and I needed an outlet. Night school and Michael became my outlets. Health issues arose too. It was a physical battle. Michael seemed refreshing and I was swept off my feet. I was indeed smitten by him. In my mind, he was a kind, loving, smart, and attentive man, who loved people. He was always lending a helping hand to someone, whether physically or verbally.

The Middle

You know, we dated for a good while. I used to love our evening car rides. We started to talk regularly on the phone. He helped me during my time of need when I was recovering from a surgery. Michael was there. The "love bombing" was laid on thick. He complimented on my beauty and personality quite often. Whenever he would talk to some of his grown children in my presence, he would tell them, "I found my wife." I was flattered at the time, but it was all moving too fast. I knew that it was "too good to be true" but I ignored the signs. I welcomed the attention. It was a distraction from the stresses in my life at the time. But then, I began noticing that we would always meet over at my house, or he would scoop me up to go on our usual outings. The outings were sweet but I'm a social butterfly. I wanted more variety. I enjoy fine dining, concerts, cultural outings, attending group events, and meeting new people. Now, I'm not saying that the person I date must do everything like me or have the same interests. I noticed that he would not be comfortable in public settings where there were large crowds. He would either become quiet or appear to be annoyed or upset. For example, Michael and I were at a local Wal-Mart picking up a few things. We were hungry and I suggested that we try a local spot. He was onboard with the idea, so I thought. Once inside, there was a small group of people waiting in line, but the line was moving. Michael's demeanor began to change. He began complaining about the line and that it was not moving fast enough. I was looking at him as if he had two heads because it was unnecessary. I kept my composure and assured him that we would get a table soon. Chiiile, this man would not stop complaining. He was irritable and wanted to leave. I was stunned and couldn't believe how he behaved. This man looked like a child having a tantrum. He had this sense of entitlement that he should not have to wait. I asked Michael if he wanted to go elsewhere, and he responded with a yes. We ended up leaving but I was pissed. The car ride was quiet, and Michael knew that I was upset with him. It didn't make sense and his behavior was unnecessary. We talked about it and Michael apologized for his behavior. I accepted his apology, but I was looking at him with the side eye. The other restaurant was quiet, no lines, and he appeared comfortable and more relaxed.

Michael and I continued to date and enjoy each other's company. However, there was an age difference of at least 10 years. The age gap did not bother me because I've always attracted older men. I began to develop feelings of love for this man and was confident that the relationship would work out. I thought the feeling was mutual because he took me around his family and close friends and paraded me around like his arm candy. There were times, many times, where he brought up the age gap. He stated that he never dated someone so young and that it was an adjustment for him. I assured him that I was comfortable with his age and that it was a first for me too. The topic of age began to decrease as time went on, so I thought, but it reared its head once more. Michael began talking about not wanting to grow older and not wanting to live past 70 years. He talked about not wanting to make me a widow with our children. When he talked about his age, he would look sad and believed that he would not live to see the age of 70. These conversations would upset me. I encouraged him to live, enjoy the moment, and God had the final say. Michael would not be easily persuaded.

Time passed on and Michael began to ghost me. He became distant, calls were decreasing, and our outings were becoming non-existent. When confronted, there was never an issue. Michael's behavior was simply baffling and confusing. I felt abandoned. I had to decide about this relationship. He was stringing me along with many empty promises. Promises that he would call or stop by. Promises that we would spend time together. It became clear that he was no longer interested. One day, we finally connected and had a serious talk about the status of our relationship and the direction that it was heading. Michael looked sad and mentioned the age gap. He did not feel comfortable and wanted me to be happy. I told him, once again, that his age did not bother me and that I loved him. He did not seem to believe that he could make me happy. At that moment, I decided to break it off. I was devastated and hurt because I felt that I was losing the love of my life in that very moment. You can't force someone to stay when you know that they've checked out. I took control of the situation and moved on.

After the break-up, there were so many emotions and thoughts running through my mind. Break-ups are not easy. I loved that man and wanted to see us win together. I had hope for us.

Pain, Pain, Go Away

Pain, Pain, Go Away; Don't
COME BACK ANOTHER DAY!
    Sleepless Nights,
    Scattered Thoughts,
    Gut Pains,
    Holding Breath,
    Restless Energy—
RELEASE THE PAIN.
    BREATHE;
JUST BREATHE.
    EXHALE.

The End

Although my relationship had ended with Michael, I still believed in us. In my heart, I believed that if it's meant to be, then it will be. So I thought, not knowing that God had a series of lessons for me that I needed to learn.

I enjoy people and love to see them happy. One summer, I had decided to have a social gathering at my house. It had been about a year since I'd seen or communicated with Michael. I'd moved on, so I thought, until he reentered my life. We didn't end on bad terms, it was drama free. Michael showed up and was low-key. He was polite and enjoyed himself with our tribe from school. As the party began to die down, Michael approached me. He professed his love for me and that he messed up. If given the opportunity, he wanted to rekindle our relationship. I still loved this man, and I began to lower my guard and reconsider allowing him back into my life.

It took some time, but eventually, Michael and I got back together. This was the start of a series of life lessons. It became a whirlwind. We fell in sync with each other as if there was no time lost between us. Hmmm, Michael had a different plan for us. As time went on, it was magical. It appeared that our love would become stronger each day. Michael began the "love bombing." Beautiful promises of marriage, children, blended families, and travel came my way regularly. I was on cloud nine; you couldn't tell me anything because my man was back! Michael spent time with me, called regularly, cooked for me, attended more social gatherings, took me to meet family and close friends, and seemed genuinely happy. The talk of our age differences was not present either. He did not mention it.

This fairytale inside my head began to unravel. It began with simply trying to help my man out. Michael was going through a personal crisis with his home and needed temporary lodging. Now, I was never one to "shack up" but I offered him temporary lodging anyway. It was dead winter, and I wanted to help him. I justified him being inside my home because we were talking about marriage. It all happened so quickly. Michael moved some clothing in and settled in rather nicely. It was awesome at first. He had a great job, he would help me, and we spent quality time together.

Fairytales do not exist but REAL LIFE does. Red flags presented themselves early in our first relationship. I overlooked many of them due to familiarity. At the time, I had fallen in love with POTENTIAL. I was "Ms. Fixer Upper" and a people pleaser. In my mind, "we all have issues and problems" but we can "work it out" together. I always gave the "benefit of the doubt" and saw the "good" in him. My actions were not healthy, and I had "Daddy Issues." Codependency developed over time with Michael. Behaviors that I'd observed and witnessed should have prevented me from entering that relationship. Michael had undesirable behaviors. Behaviors demonstrated: *Erratic Driving *Explosive Temper with Others *Unrealistic Sense of Entitlement *Bad-Mouthed Past Relationships *Gossiper *Hung Around Serial Cheaters (Close Friends & Family) *Excessive Apologies for Undesirable Behaviors *Strained Relationships with Some Adult Children *Abandoned Fatherly Duties *Empty Promises *Blamed Others *Didn't Own or Rent Property *Unstable *No Consistency *Mommy Issues *Lacked Empathy.

When Michael and I reconnected again, he was put in the position of control. He initiated this relationship the second time around. It was all peaches and cream, until we lived together. Michael had placed me on a high pedestal and wanted me to behave in such a particular manner. He jokingly said that he wanted me to look "pretty" and be "quiet." Michael didn't like a "loud" woman. He wanted all my attention focused on him. I noticed that he became "clingy" and "smothering." I can recall a time where he took over the television and wanted me to watch certain shows with him. Sometimes I would keep him company but there were times when I just needed "me time" and wanted to do my own thing. There were times when this action would irritate him. It was draining to expect me to be right underneath him. I always was a go-getter and had various interests and hobbies that I enjoyed. Michael would question me if I would stay later than usual from work or if I hung out too late with one of my close friends. Behaviors were subtle at first due to his "joking" manner but in the back of my mind, I took note of it. One time, he jokingly mentioned that he would "cut" me. On many occasions, I would confront him and not take his jokes lightly. Michael did not like confrontation. Often, he would give me the silent treatment or ghost me in my own house. I felt like I had to walk on eggshells in my own house! One concern that I noticed with him was that he began to stay in the house for long periods of time. His temperament changed too. Michael became moody and withdrawn. When confronted, he was "fine." He had a great job and then it went downhill. It was not pleasant to watch him go from a well-paying full-time job to no job in a matter of months. It felt as if Michael wanted me to take care of him financially. That was not going to happen; he would have to pull his own weight. He had to get a job, so he found something part-time to keep the peace in the household. There were many inconsistencies, and I would question him a lot. His stories became suspect and not credible. Gaslighting became prevalent in our relationship. Michael had me second-guessing and scratching my head multiple times, but I knew that I wasn't crazy with my feelings.

Changes had to be made, so I had a long talk with God. I asked God to remove this man from my life. I was drained and reached my endpoint. I did not want to marry this type of man. I wanted so much more for my life. I was worthy and deserved a healthy relationship.

God moved with such a quickness that it left me speechless. Michael walked out of my life within the same week! His rejection was God's protection. Immediately, darkness turned to light!

The Undeniable Strength of a Woman resonates within me. It is my belief that God places us in situations and relationships to help us grow. Lessons must be taught for us to learn.

Spending time alone with God and myself has strengthened and changed my perspective. I've learned that I do matter and I know my self-worth. God does not want his children to suffer.

This relationship taught me great lessons that are embedded within me, lessons that I do not take lightly. The wisdom that I gained from these lessons is preparing me for healthier relationships. Lessons learned from this experience:

- I deserve healthy relationships.
- I know my value.
- I know my self-worth.
- I love myself.
- Do not overlook Red Flags.
- Rely on God for guidance.
- Have faith in God & believe that it will work out for the greater good.
- Do not settle for mediocrity.
- Establish & maintain set boundaries.
- Trust my discernment.
- Find the power in my voice.
- Follow gut instincts.

- Observe actions and not just face value…when someone shows you who they are, believe them.
- Protect my peace.
- Guard my energy.
- Forgive, pray for them, & move on.
- Do not dim my God-given light.

There are no regrets! I had to go through this type of relationship in order to grow. Since leaving this relationship, I started living again and thriving. Opportunities became bountiful. God brought me through, and I came out a stronger woman. My pain flowed deeply but was washed away. Better days were coming.

Gentle Rain

Gentle Rain,
Tears fallin' down my face
    Like a gentle rain,
    Slowly and wet.

Each teardrop is a soft caress,
    Soothing away my pain
    That's deep down
    In my soul.

Gentle Rain,
Gently fallin' down my face
    To help ease the pain.

The pain of souls not yet united.

Gentle Rain
Fallin' down around me
    Like a light blanket
    Sheltering **all** of "me,"
    Protecting me.

Gentle Rain
Sheltering and protecting all of me
    Until
    It turns into
    A
    Mist,
    Then
    SUNSHINE.

Beautiful Women, you are deserving of healthy relationships. No one has the right to mistreat you emotionally, psychologically, physically, sexually, verbally, or economically. Know your worth and believe that there are sunny days ahead.

Sunny Days

Sunny Days
    Are up ahead.
Sunny Days
    Are freedom.
Sunny Days
    Take the pain away.
Sunny Days
    Bring back life.
Sunny Days

Bring forth energy and light.
Sunny Days
Restore faith, energy, and light.
Sunny Days
Restore LOVE.
Sunny Days
Restore PEACE.

Domestic Violence continues to rise and affect women daily. If you or someone you know suffers in silence, help is just a phone call away. Call the National Domestic Violence Hotline: 1-800-799-SAFE (7233); TTY (1-800-787-3224) or Text "START" to 88788.

Kimmoly K. LaBoo is a Published Author, International Speaker and Certified Master Life Coach. She is at the helm of LaBoo Publishing Enterprise, as CEO and founder. She is a highly respected change agent in her community and around the world.

Her award-winning company was created for the independent self-publisher. Kimmoly enjoys providing expert guidance and unlimited support to her clients, helping them recognize their brilliance, sharing their stories with the world, as writers.

She has dedicated her life to serving girls and women through mentoring, and coaching. Her compassionate coaching style, challenges clients to embrace change and show up confidently, using their unique gifts and talents to impact and serve others.

She was named among the Top 25 Women in Business by Courageous Woman magazine. She has appeared on Think Tech Hawaii, WPB Networks, Heaven 600, ABC2News, FOX5 News, and has graced many stages speaking and training to include, Department of Veterans Affairs, Blacks in Government National Training Conference, and Coppin State University.

Kimmoly is the mother of two amazing sons and currently resides in Maryland.

Contact Information:
www.laboopublishing.com
staff@laboopublishing.com

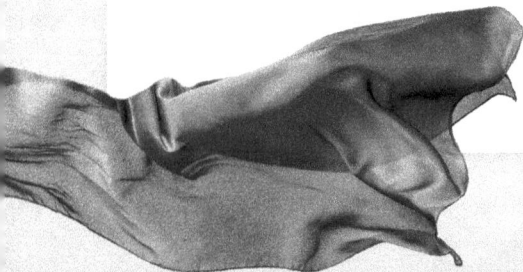

When It's All Said and Done

Kimmoly La Boo

Now that you've read our stories, I know that you have many of your own. I want to challenge you. Take a moment to think about your past. What have you had to overcome? Have you actually overcome it or are you still holding on to it, pretending you've let it go?

List 3-5 major game changers in your life. What has happened to you in your past that is hindering you from living up to your full potential? I challenge you to be honest with yourself. Honesty breeds freedom from bondage.

Close your eyes and begin to think back to those situations that have contributed to who you are this very moment. List them here:

1. _____

2. _____

3. _____

4. _____

5. _____

Look over your list. Are there people tied to each of these situations listed that you need to forgive? I know you may be asking yourself, "How do I forgive someone who was unfaithful, or someone who raped or molested me? How do I forgive someone who violated my trust in a major way?" Perhaps you are placing your blame a little higher and you have an issue that you are blaming God for. The longer you hold on to un-forgiveness, the longer you are bound. "What do you mean by that?" you might ask. Well, if you refuse to forgive someone who has bruised you, you will remain broken. Forgiveness is not about the other person. Forgiveness is for you. When you release a person (forgiving them) you free a part of yourself that was so focused on that person that it was consuming a part of your unconscious mind. When you choose not to forgive, you choose to carry extra baggage; there is a price to pay for that. When you make a decision to forgive, you make the decision to live again.

Rediscovering You

As women we often get lost somewhere along the way. We care for and protect everyone else. We make things look easy while we shelter our pain. Some of us need to find our way back to us. While it is great that you have figured out how to juggle your role as mom, wife, sister, daughter, friend, and employee, it is important not to lose the core of who you are. If you struggle to even think of what your purpose is outside of the many hats that you wear or what success would look like for you after you have exhausted all of those roles, after the kids are grown, after the divorce or death of a spouse, after retirement; who will you be? Lots of women feel exhausted and empty after they have poured everything out of their cup for everyone else. Perhaps you need to find your purpose (again) and create a new path to what success looks like for you.

Finding Your Purpose Again

What do you do well? What do other people tell you that you do well? This is often helpful in defining your purpose. Often, others can see in you what you cannot or will not see in yourself. For example, if people always talk about how great your desserts are and they say things like, "You should have your own bakery," perhaps you should, or if people are always saying, "you have the gift of gab," maybe you are supposed to be spreading a message far and wide with your voice. Pay attention to the positive things people say about you. If you really want to find out what you were born to do, ask the one who created you. God gave every single one of us a gift. Every person was born to solve a problem here on earth. You have a purpose, and it is not that hard to figure it out.

Lots of people struggle for years trying to find their purpose. Pay attention to yourself. Get to know yourself. What are you passionate about? Your passion is likely to reveal your purpose. It could be what you love to do, or it may be something that bothers you immensely. What is your pet peeve? What is it that makes your heart ache because it isn't right? Perhaps you can't stand to see elderly people mistreated. Maybe you don't like what has become of our teenagers. You could be bothered by the whole political process. Listen to what your senses are telling you and you will know what your purpose is.

Part of knowing what you are good at doing comes from knowing what you are not good at doing. Take a moment to list your strengths and weaknesses. None of us really like to think about the things we don't do well. Nonetheless, I urge you to complete this exercise. Once you are done identifying these two categories you will be able to focus on your strengths and acknowledge your weaknesses and begin to work on them. Knowing both and acknowledging them are necessary for your success. I challenge you to really spend time developing the list below. Perhaps these examples will help you get started.

Strengths	Weaknesses
Organized	Procrastinator
Detail Oriented	Time Management
Great Communicator	Perfectionist

Creating a Path to Success

I've encountered many trials in my life. There were times when I had no idea what the next step, hour, day, or month would look like but I had to rely on my faith in God. During those times when I thought I would not make it through the storm, He carried me every step of the way. When I was filled with sadness, un-forgiveness, bitterness and anger, I had to learn to lean on the Lord. When there was no one else there for me to turn to, when I felt I had lost everything, He was right there to comfort me. He was there to hold me up when I couldn't physically or mentally care for myself. I would like to share with you the path that led me to success, and I pray that it will help you to overcome and embrace the life you were always destined to live.

1. **Jeremiah 29:11.** *"For I know the plans I have for you," declares the LORD, "plans to prosper you and not to harm you, plans to give you hope and a future."*

   Often we try to do things our way and we mess everything up. We stray from the perfect will of God. It is when we are outside of the will of God that we experience our greatest turmoil. Trust that God's plan is perfect for your life and stop trying to make it what you want it to be. God has the ultimate plan for your life.

2. **Matthew 6:33.** *But seek ye first the kingdom of God, and his righteousness; and all these things shall be added unto you.*

   Often we try to obtain things. We focus on the tangible instead of the intangible. If we would just focus on the things of God and His Kingdom, the Word tells us that all those things we are trying to gain in our own strength will be added unto us.

3. **Luke 6:37.** *Judge not, and ye shall not be judged: condemn not, and ye shall not be condemned, forgive, and ye shall be forgiven.*

   It took me years to walk in this concept because I had been hurt by so many people. It was not easy by any means. The Lord kept speaking to my spirit, telling me to forgive, and I could not. At one point in my life, I held myself in bondage for three years, unwilling to forgive. When I finally surrendered and did what God had asked me to do, which was to stop judging and to forgive someone who had hurt me deeply, I was freed. It seemed like in an instant everything that God had wanted to pour into my life was immediately released. If this is an area you are struggling with, I implore you, forgive and free yourself from the chains with which you are confining yourself.

4. **Psalm 55:22** *Cast thy burden upon the LORD, and he shall sustain thee: he shall never suffer the righteous to be moved.*

As women we tend to carry a lot of baggage that is not ours to carry. The word of God tells us to cast our burdens upon the Lord. He is far better equipped to handle them than we are.

5. **Proverbs 3:5-6.** *Trust in the Lord with all your heart; and don't lean on your own understanding. In all things acknowledge him, and he shall direct your way.*

This passage of scripture simply tells us if we trust Him, He will show us the way. That's awesome. After years of trying to figure it out on my own, I've found that He is much better at navigating my life than I ever was. Why don't you let Him direct your path? He will take you to places you never dreamed you could go.

6. **Romans 1:17.** *And Jesus said unto them, "If ye have faith as a grain of mustard seed, ye shall say unto this mountain, Remove hence to yonder place; and it shall remove; and nothing shall be impossible to you."*

During those times when life was very difficult for me, I felt like I was down to a tiny grain the size of a mustard seed in my faith, but I was never completely without it. In hindsight, I now know that nothing was impossible for me to achieve or to overcome. I thank God that all He required of me during that time was mustard seed-size faith. As a result I now have tremendous faith. I encourage you today to hold on to your faith even when things look horrible. God will see you through.

7. **Matthew 19:26** *But Jesus beheld them, and said unto them, with men this is impossible; but with God all things are possible.*

Moving from victim to victor requires faith, determination, perseverance, and a strength that is not your own, *but with God all things are possible.*

Take a Moment to Relax

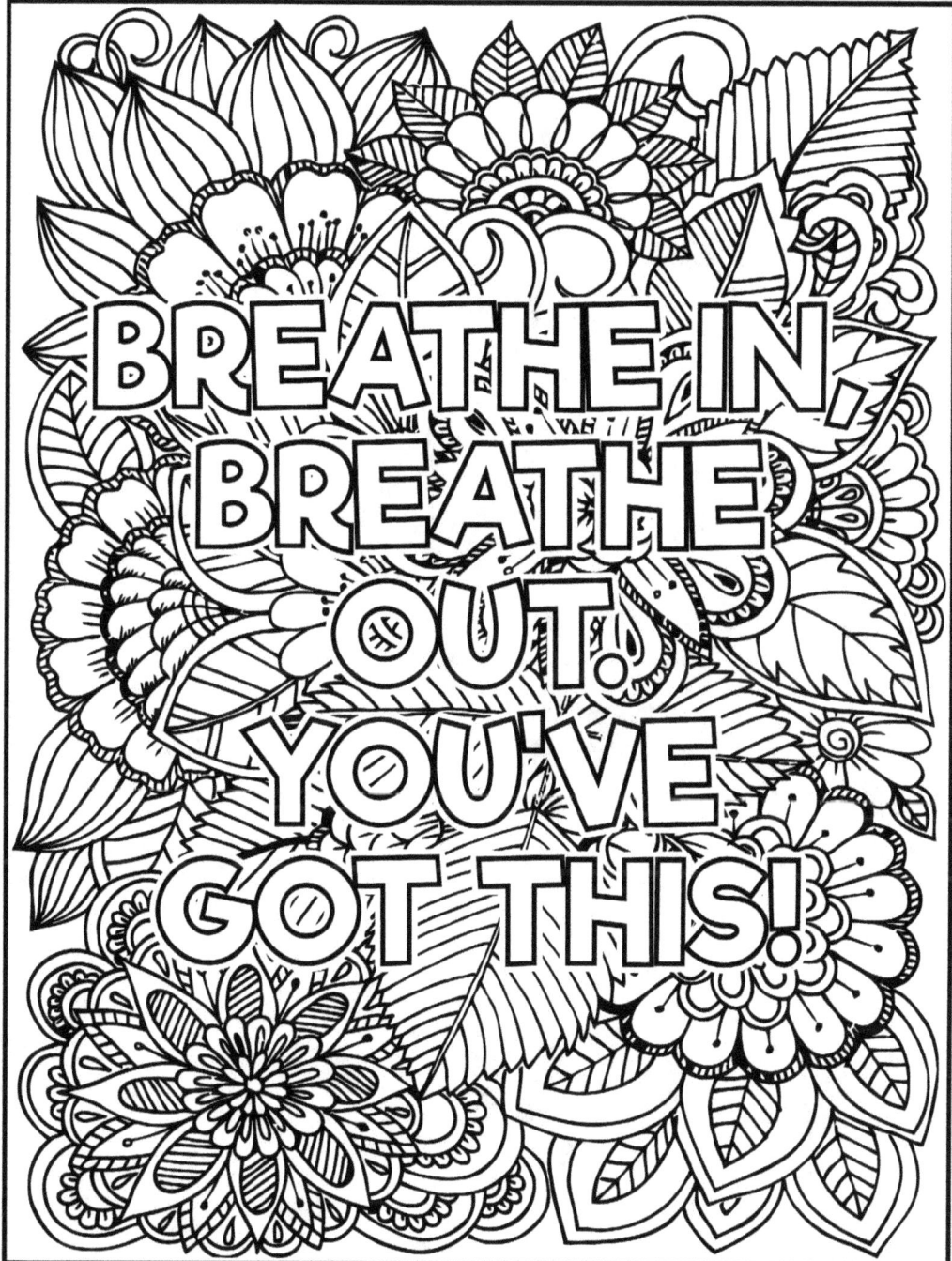

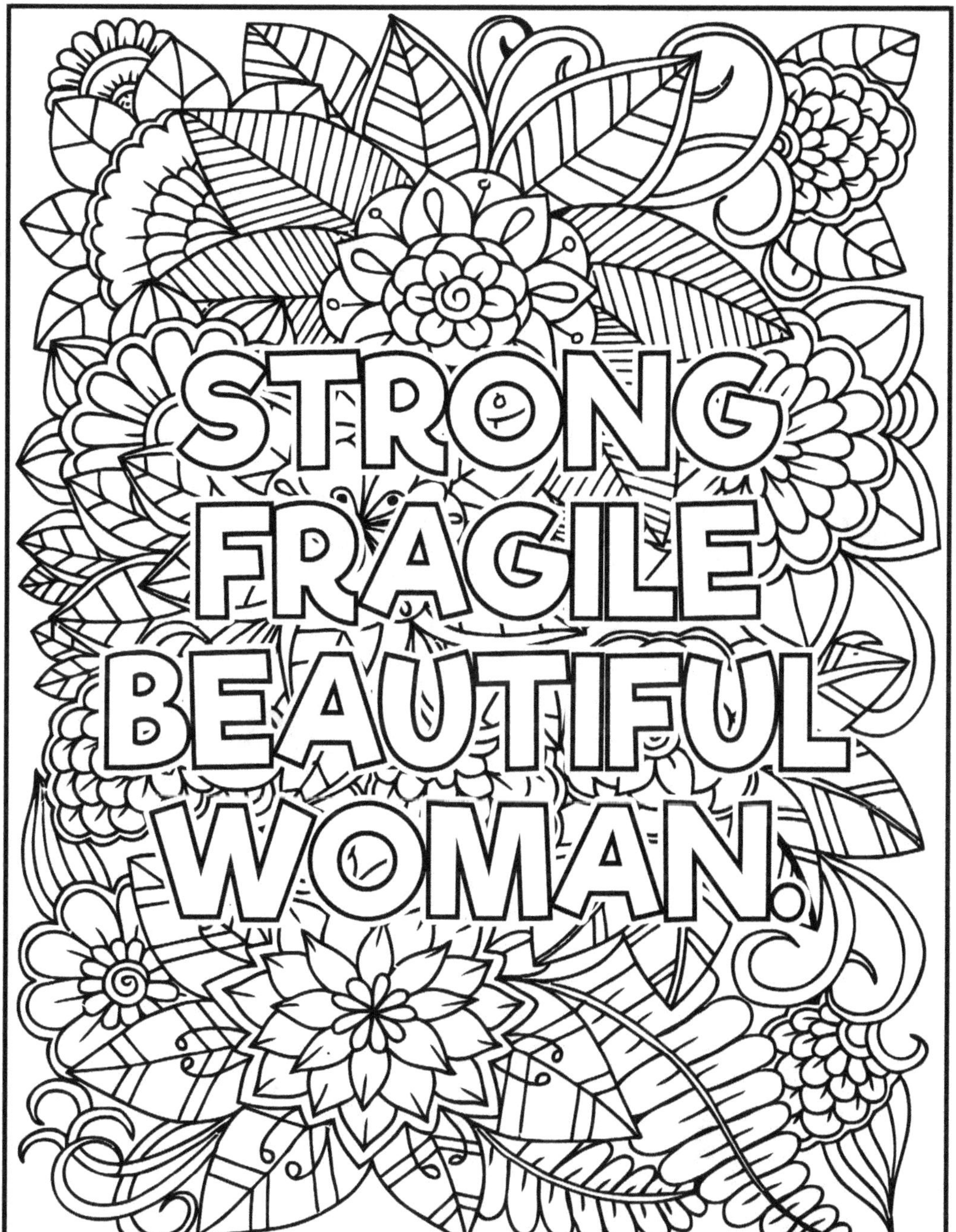
STRONG
FRAGILE
BEAUTIFUL
WOMAN.

IF IT COSTS YOU YOUR PEACE, IT'S TOO EXPENSIVE

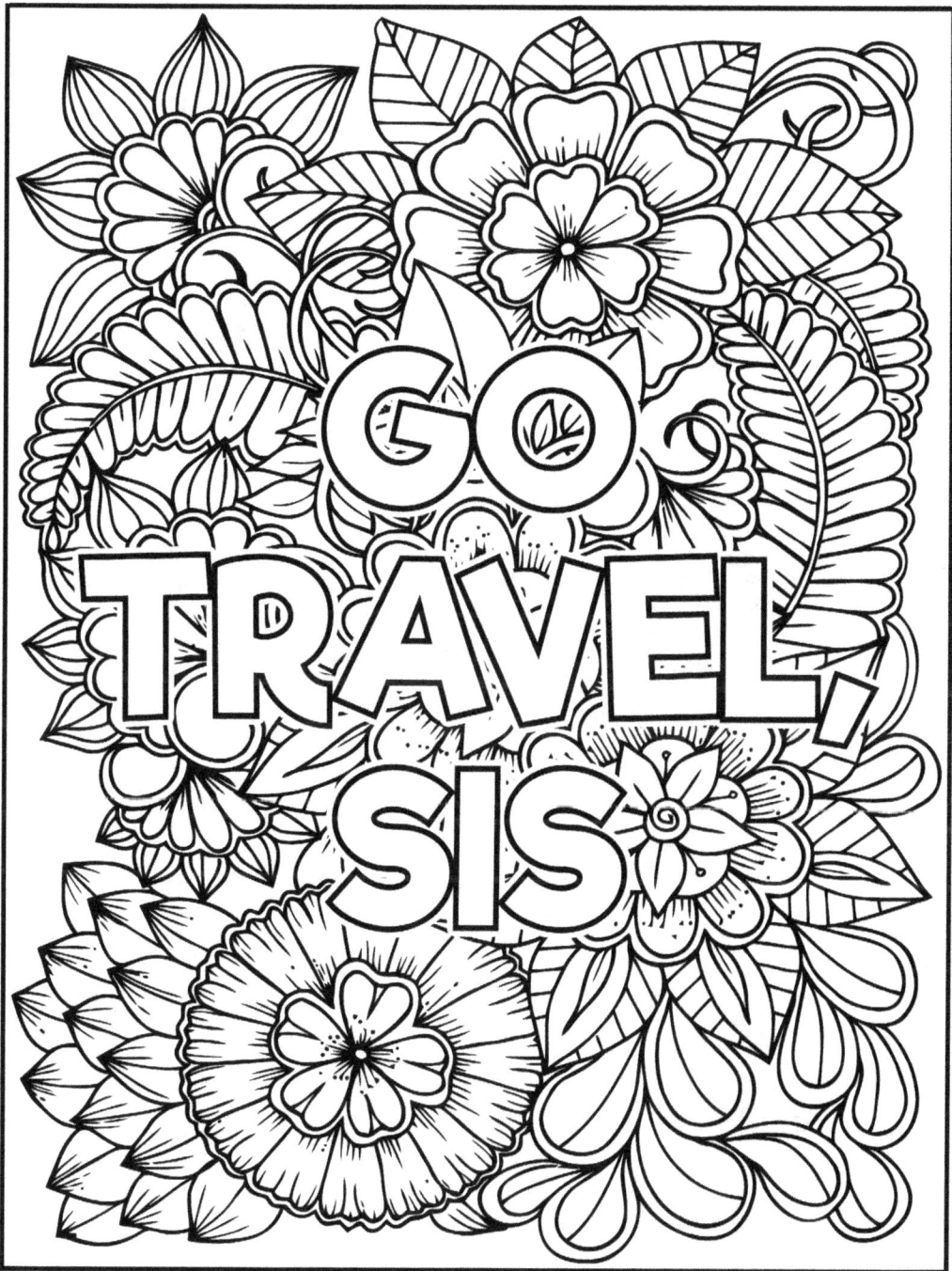

ASK FOR HELP IF YOU NEED IT

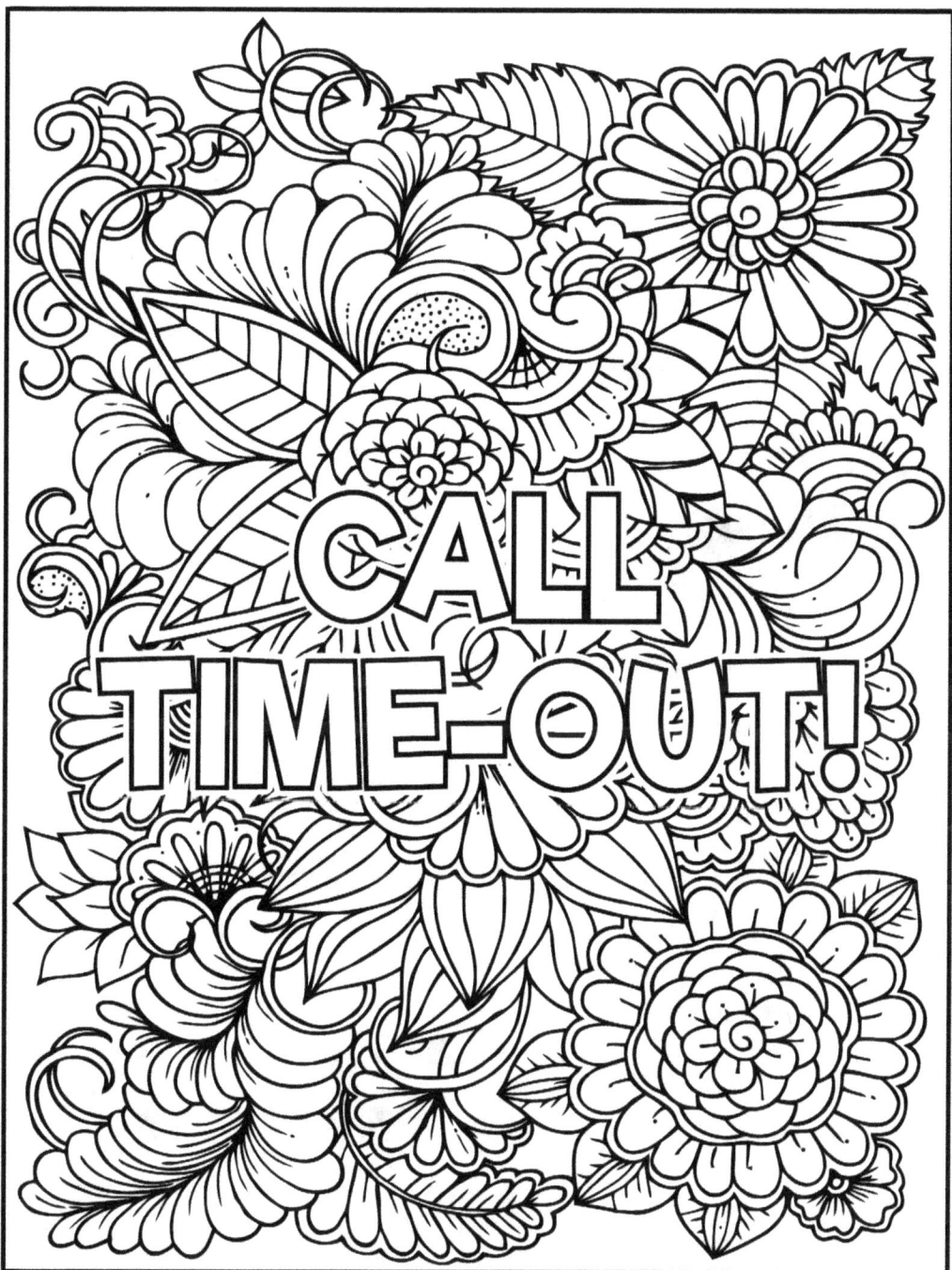

CALL TIME-OUT!

YOU ARE POWERFUL BEYOND MEASURE

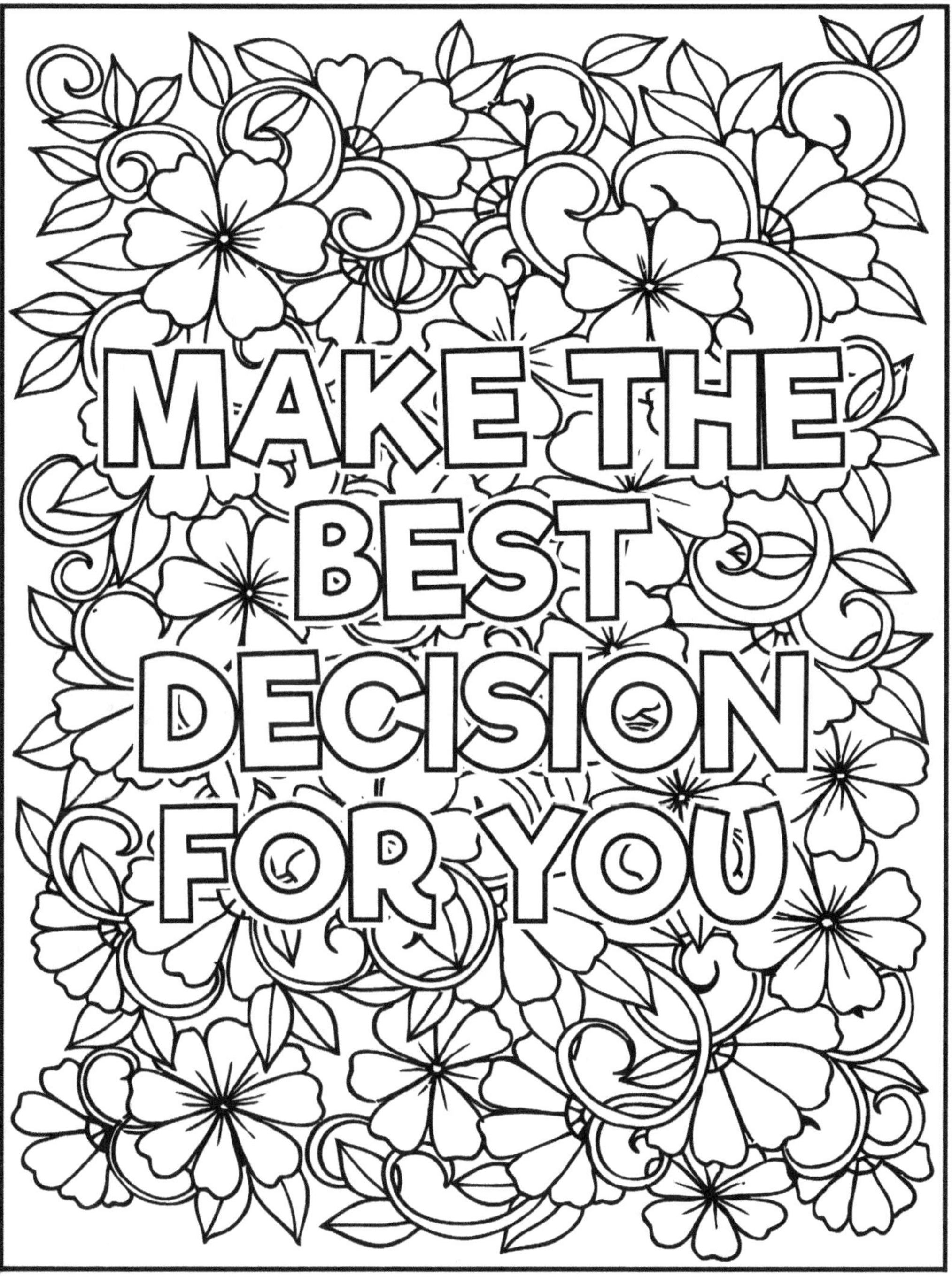
MAKE THE
BEST
DECISION
FOR YOU

WORD SEARCH

Instructions: Can you find all of the words hidden in the puzzle? Words can be down, across or diagonal.

```
G P H G Q S A A V X T O N H M
B G Z A F R L Z M A S S A G E
Z O A R I A Q E F C B U L A M
V A E S S N P K E I A R A T E
C O Q T O B Y U A P L U V A N
B I D Y M P Q A F S A J Z C T
C Z O I A O I U R T N U C V A
I I R R E A J T Q F C G K A L
Z J E N D I E H H X E E O C H
A H R E A D I N G U O E T A E
T X E X E R C I S E W U E T A
C R S M M L Q A U A A U A I L
A I E W L A R E A A T V L O T
O W D S B E N G J G E R I N H
K T L J T N A L Y U R A E U A
```

WORDS TO FIND

- [ ] MENTAL HEALTH
- [ ] VACATION
- [ ] MASSAGE
- [ ] READING
- [ ] THERAPY
- [ ] EXERCISE
- [ ] BALANCE
- [ ] WATER
- [ ] SLEEP
- [ ] REST

www.ingramcontent.com/pod-product-compliance
Lightning Source LLC
Chambersburg PA
CBHW052042270326
41931CB00012B/2596